Critters to Color
By Robin Joy Andreae

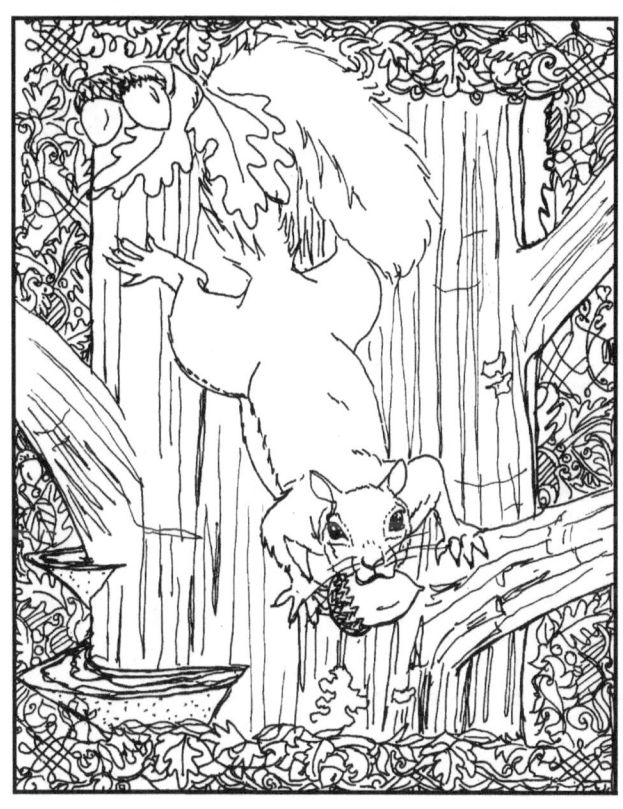

Copyright 2016 Robin Joy Andreae
ISBN 10:1523717742

ISBN 13:9781523717743

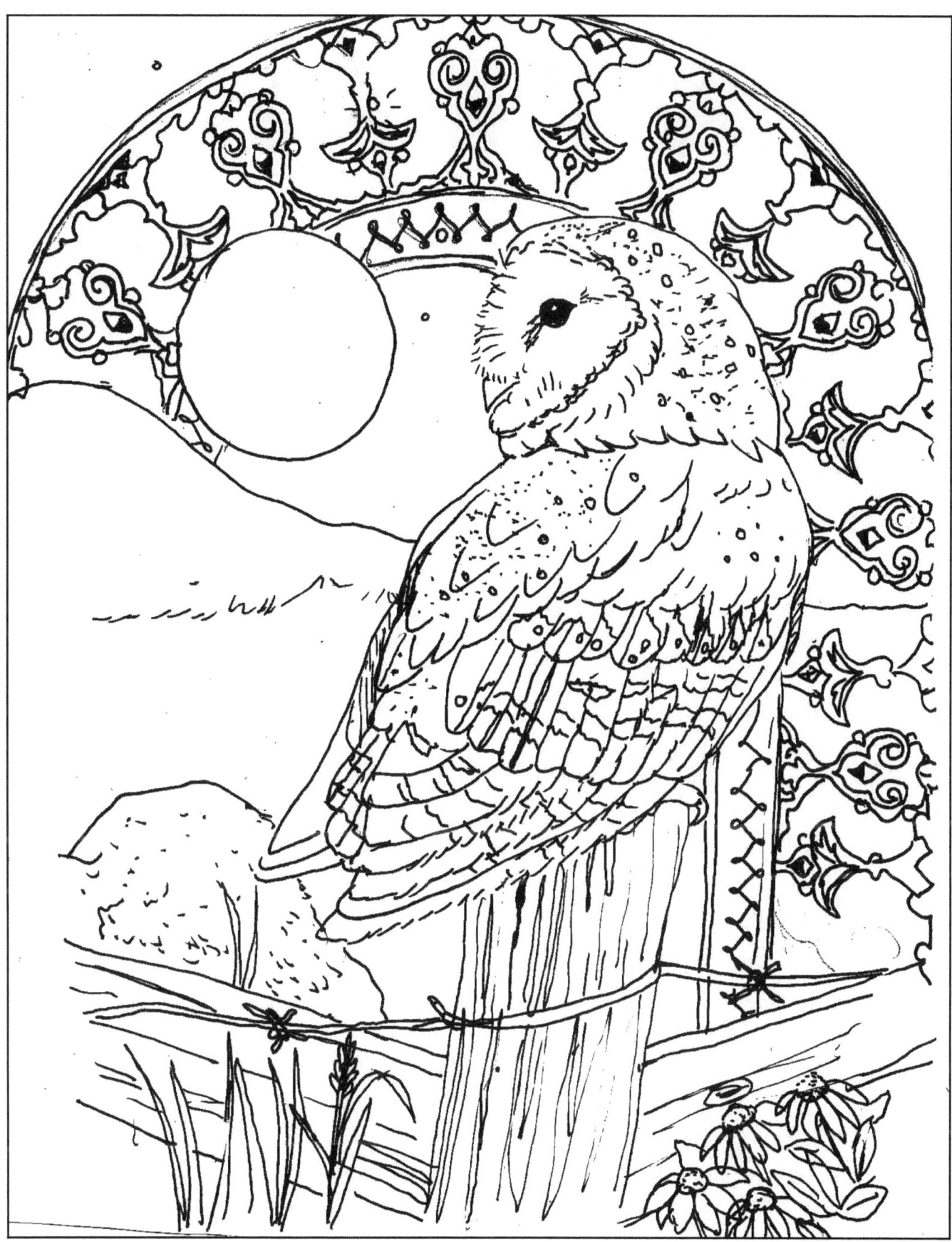

Figure 1 Barn Owl

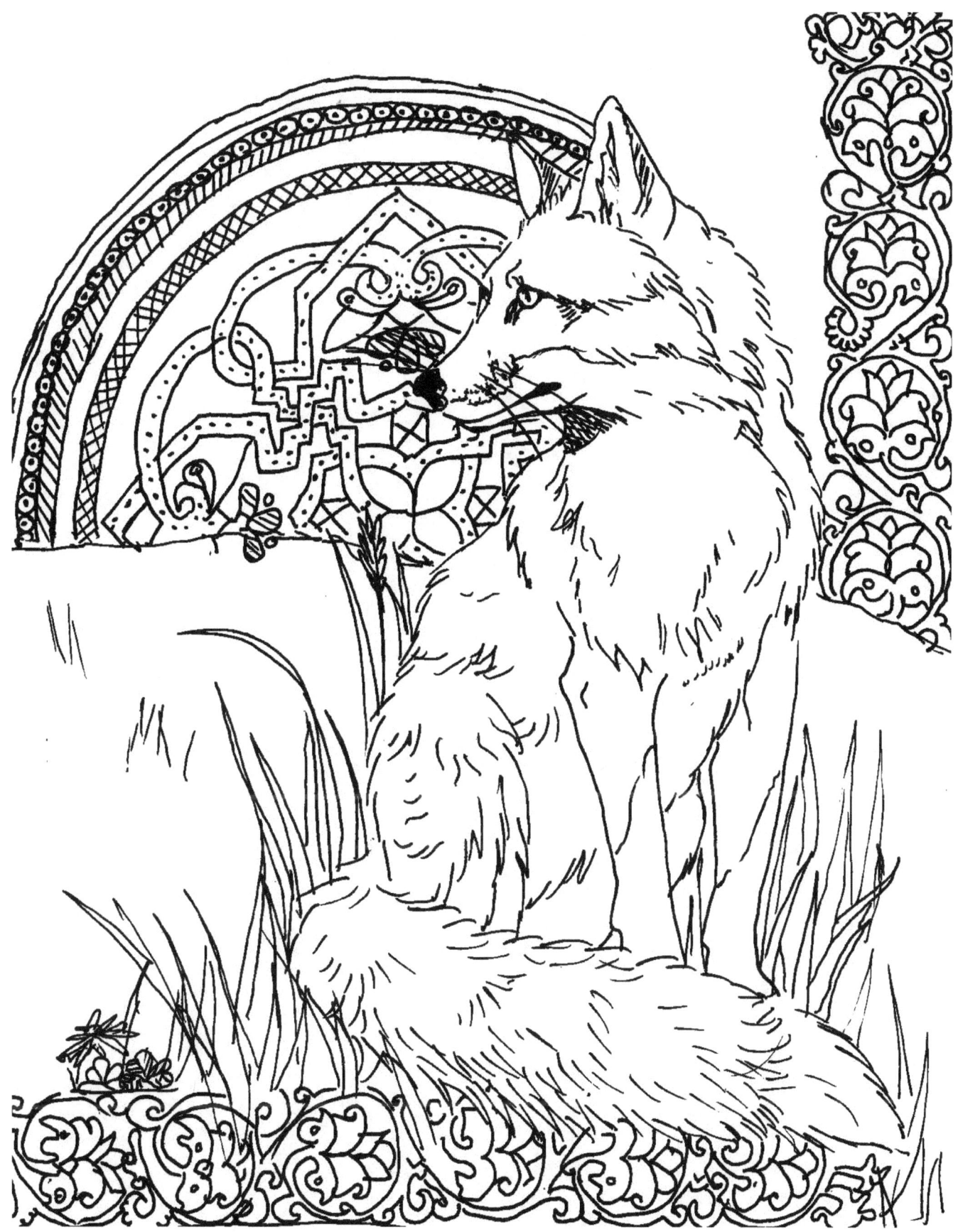

Figure 2 Red Fox

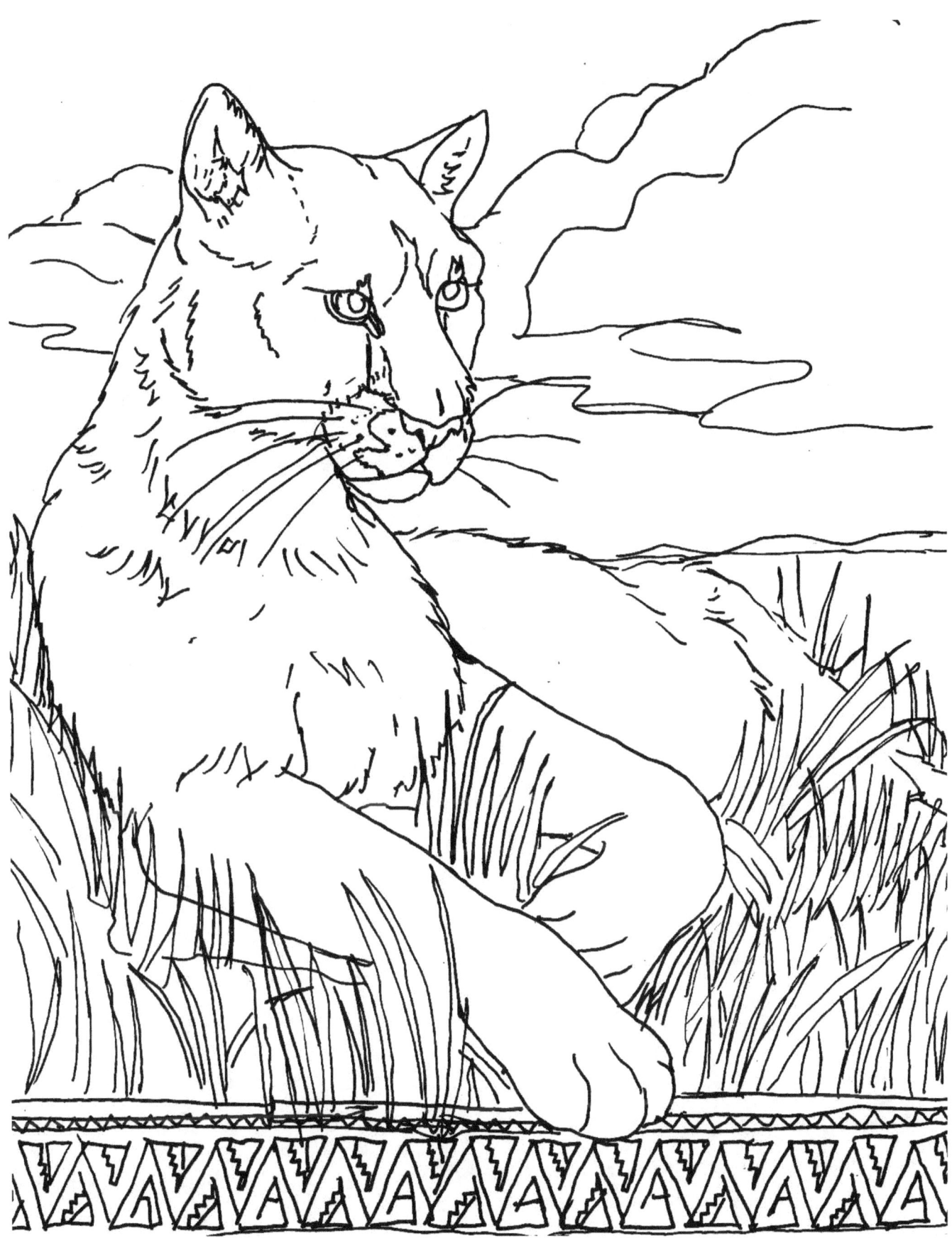

Figure 3 Mountain Lion

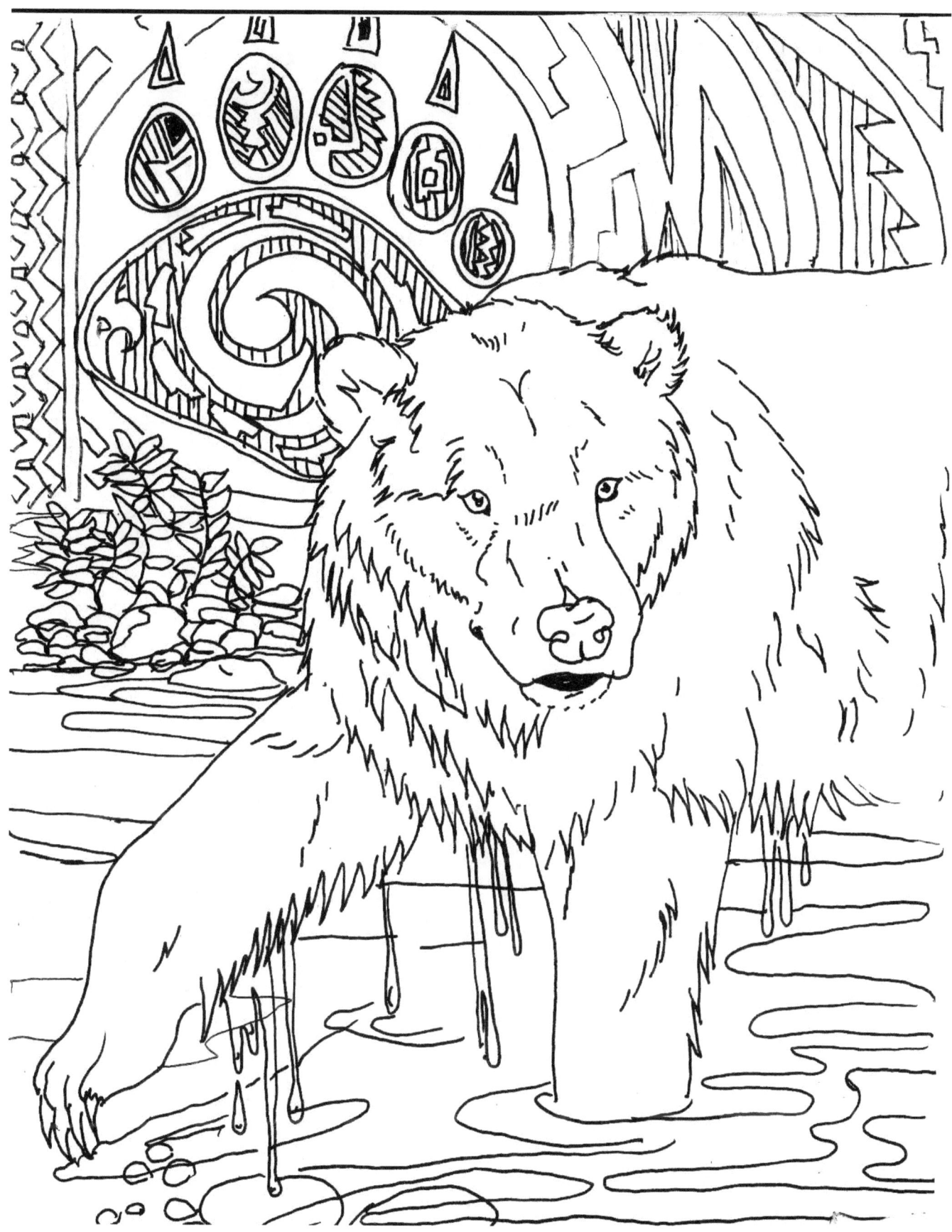

Figure 4 Brown Bear

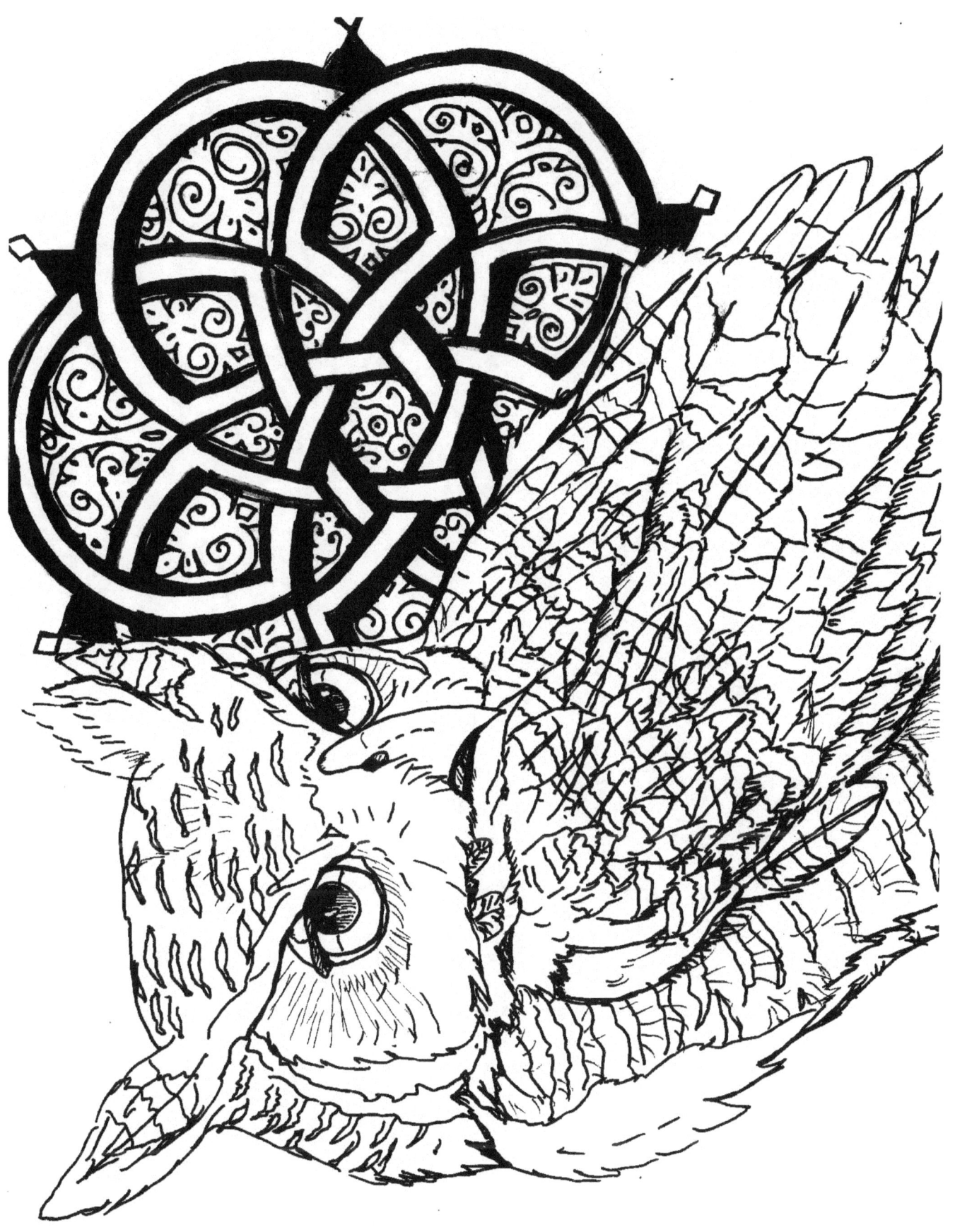

Figure 5 Great Horned Owl

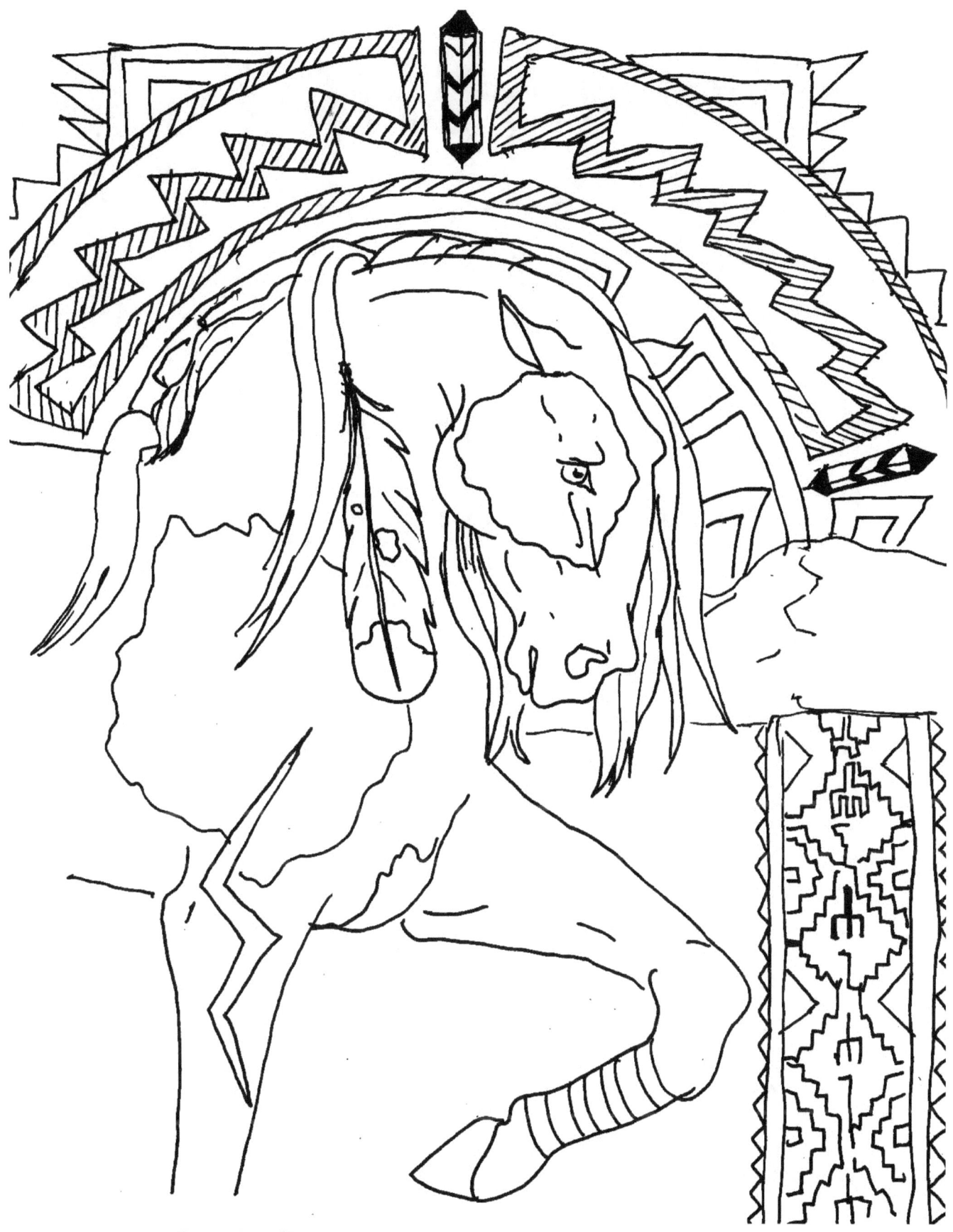

Figure 6 Paint Horse

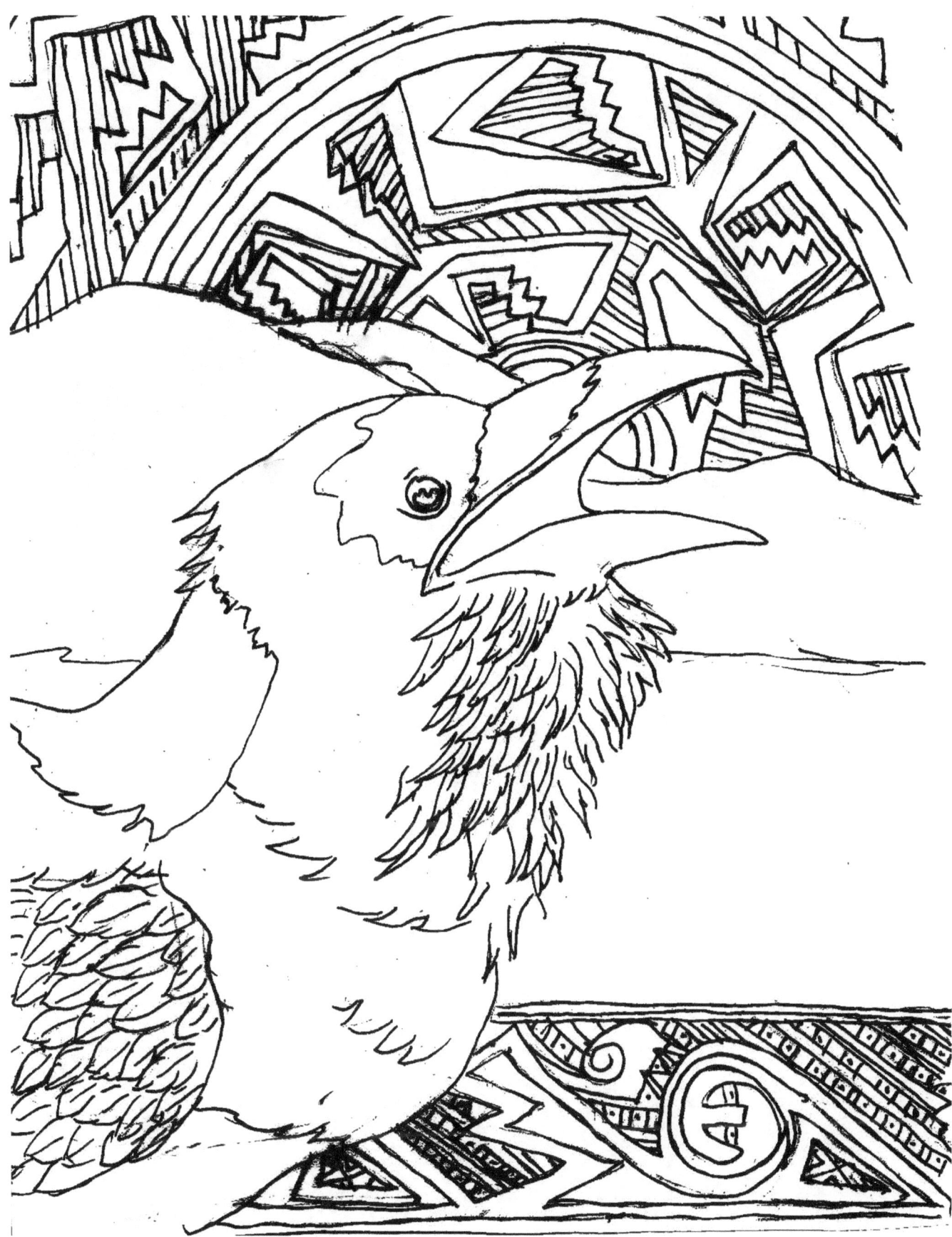

Figure 7 Raven

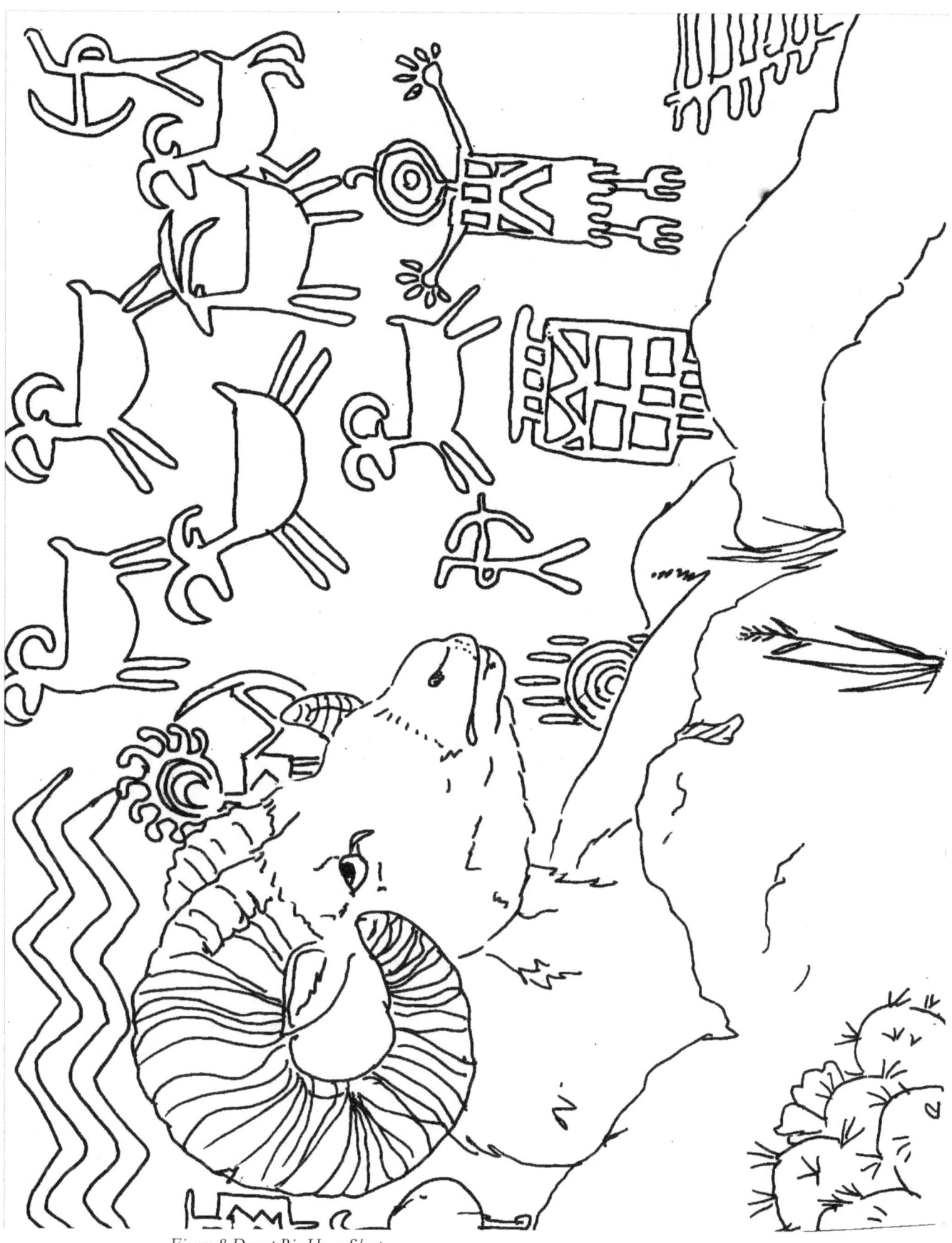

Figure 8 Desert Big Horn Sheep

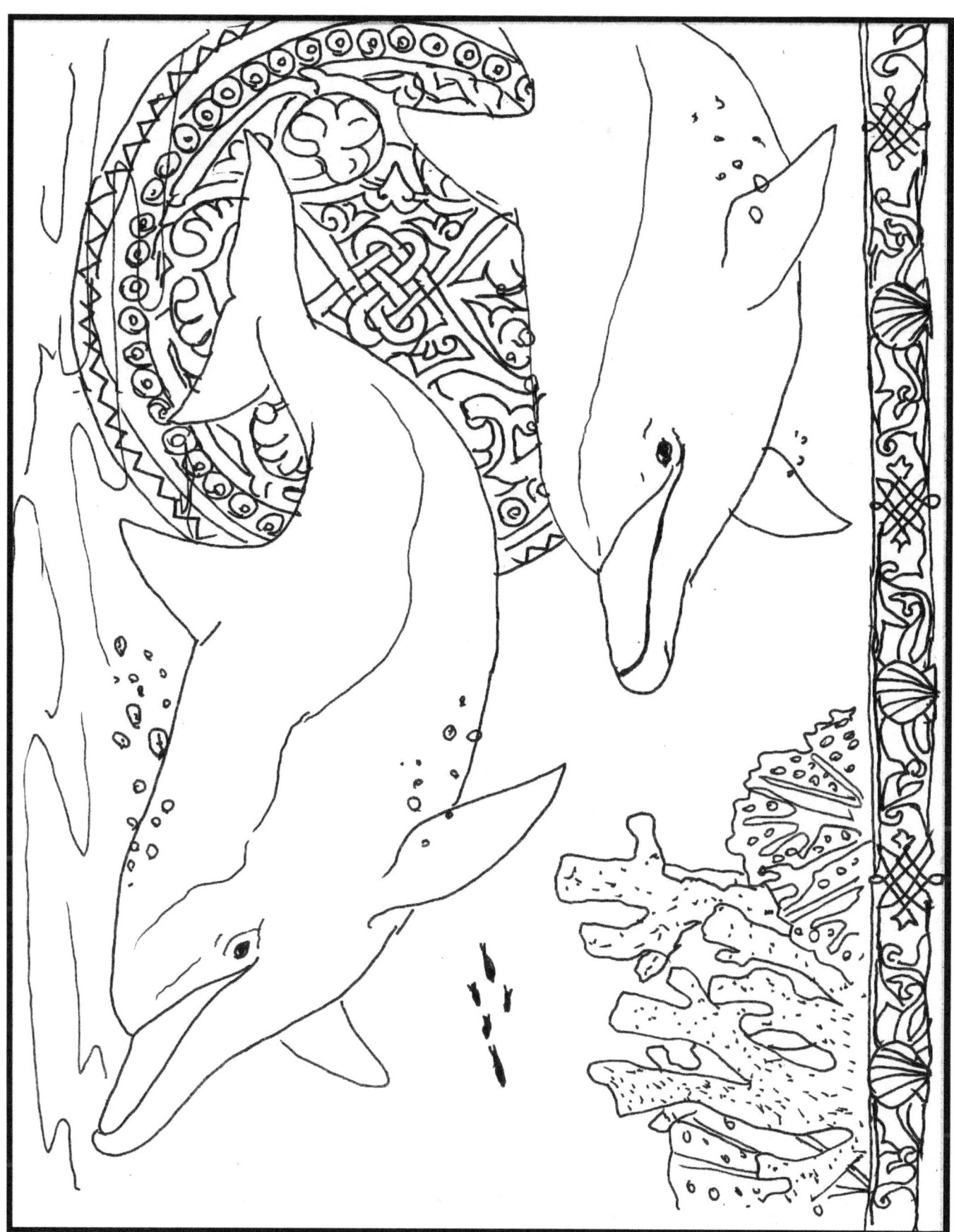

Figure 9 Bottlenose Dolphins

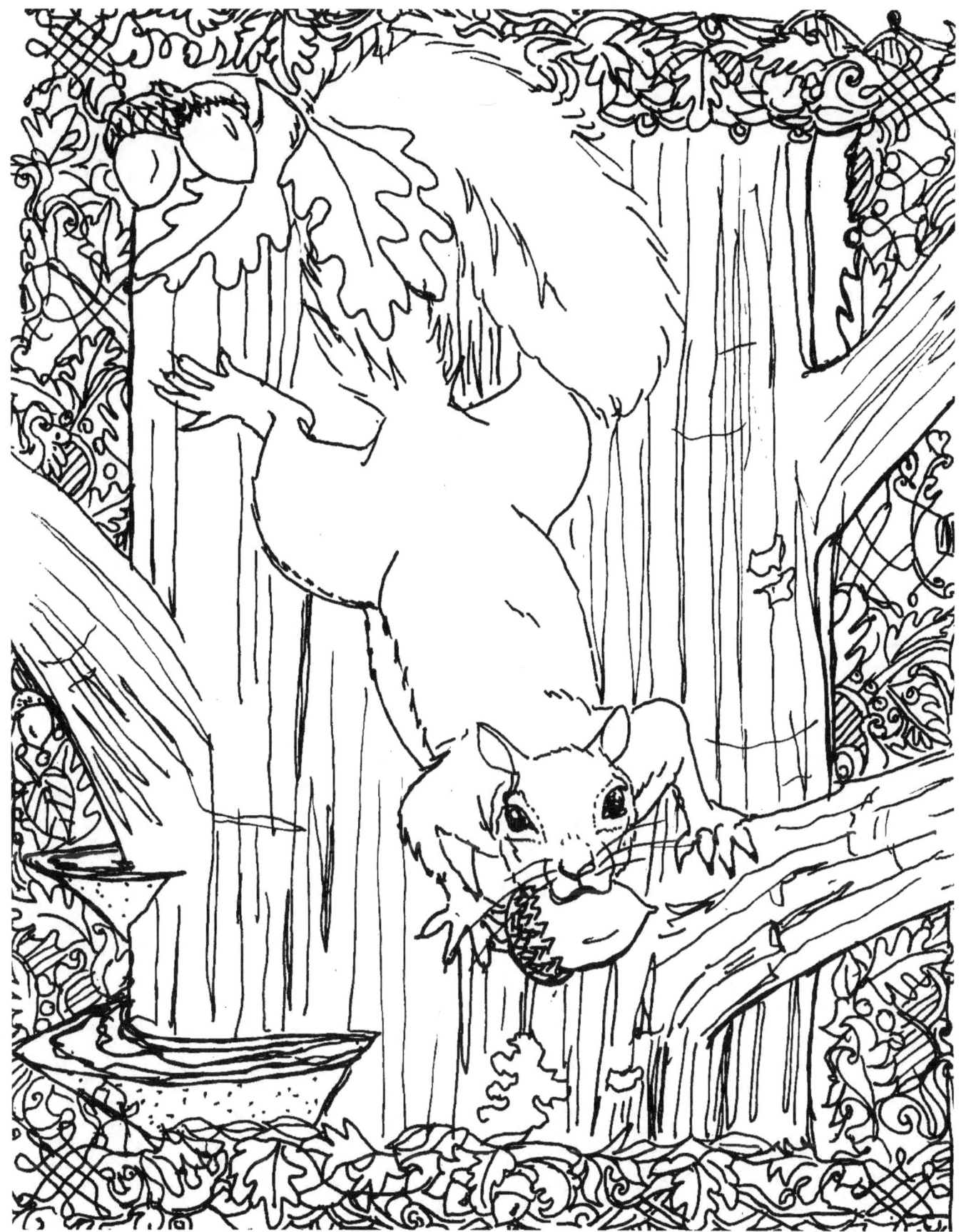

Figure 10 Red Squirrel

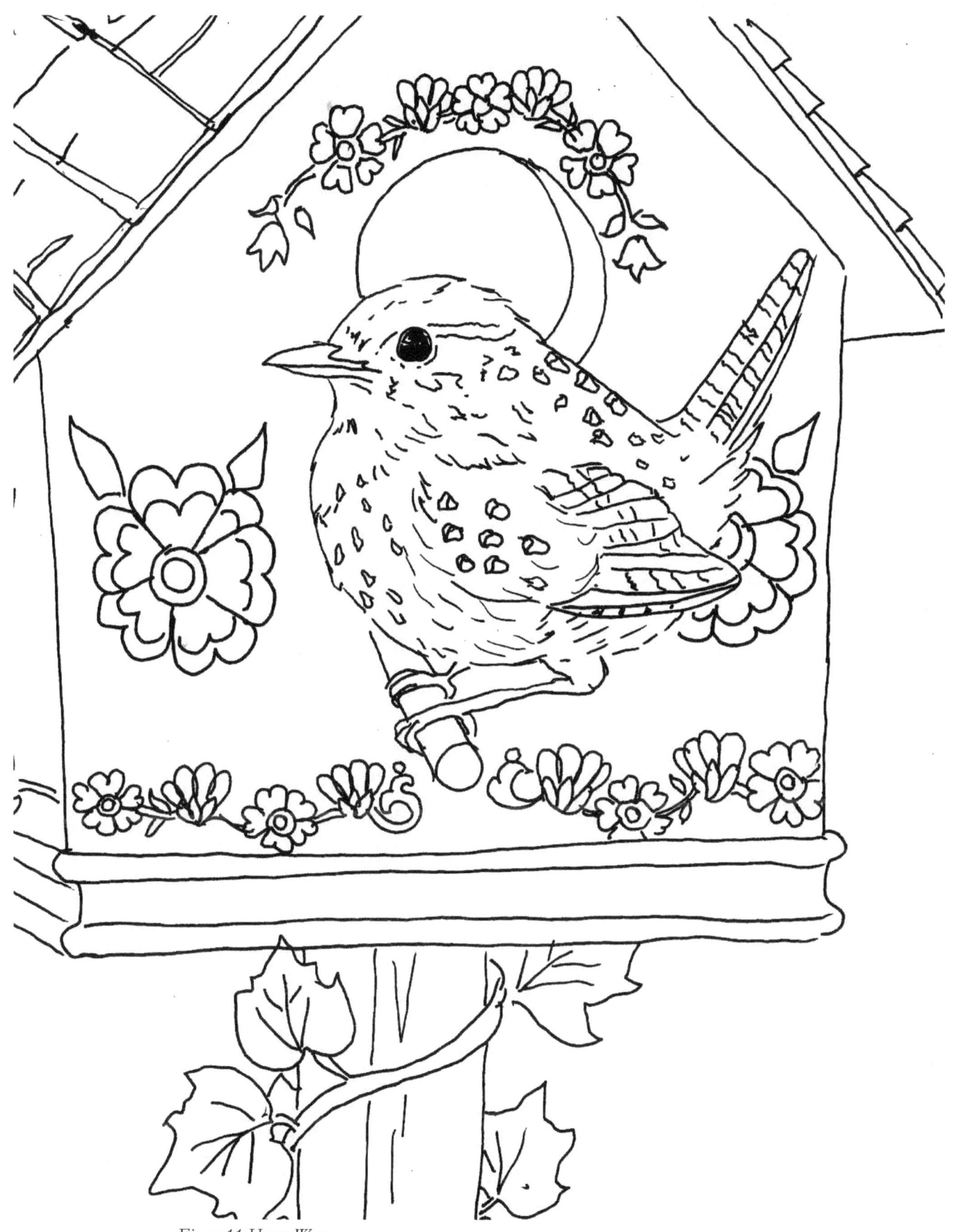

Figure 11 House Wren

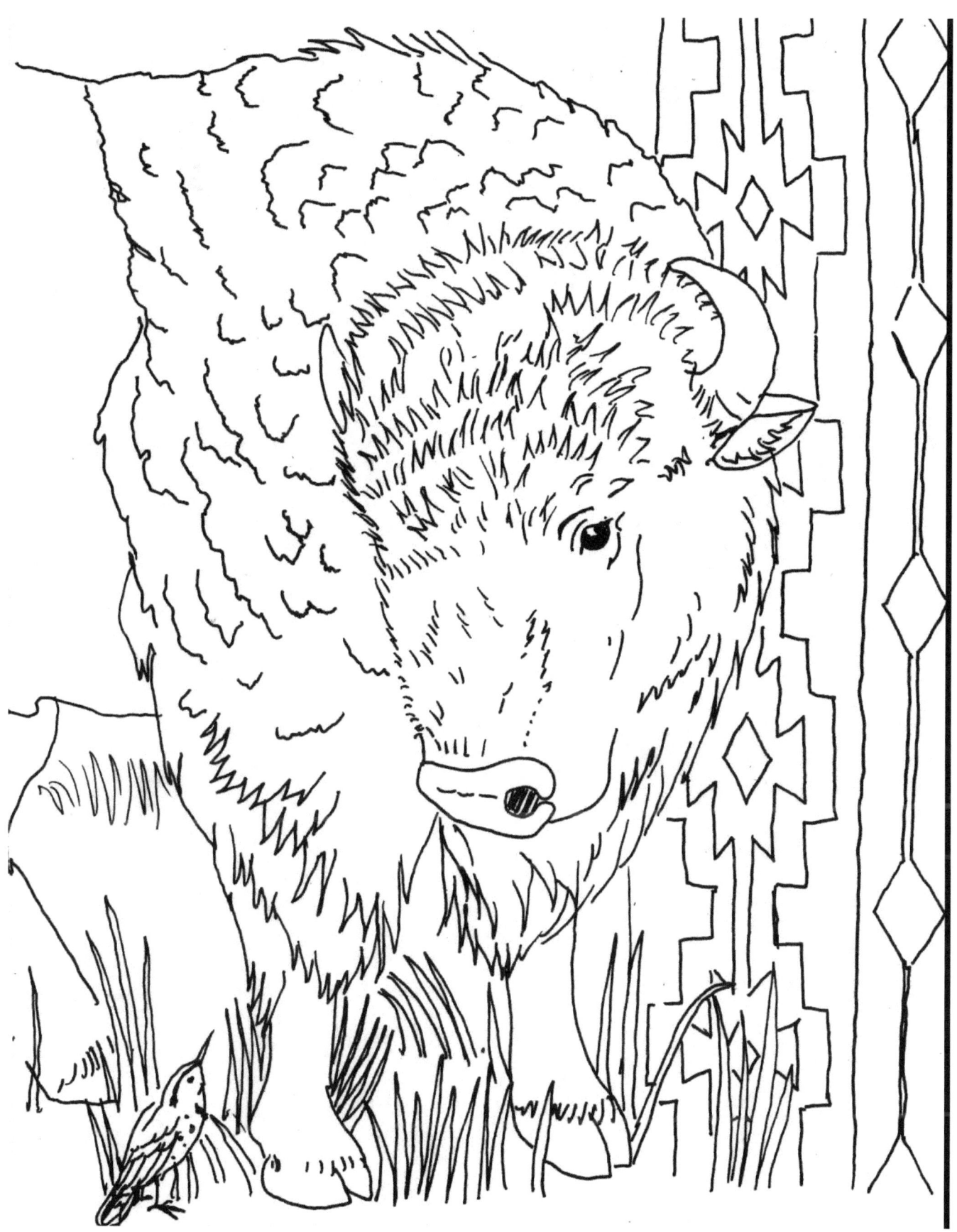

Figure 12 American Bison & Meadowlark

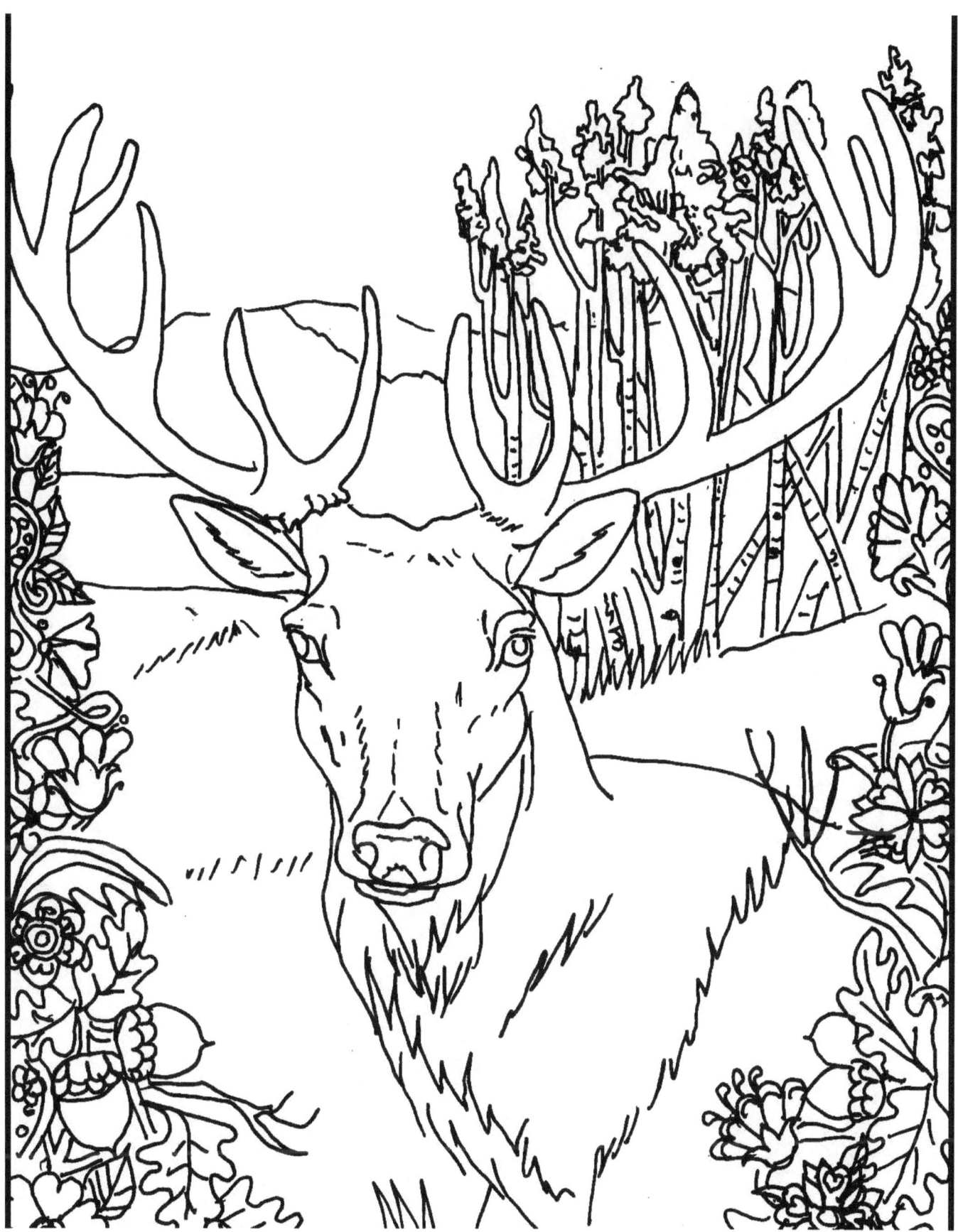

Figure 13 Elk

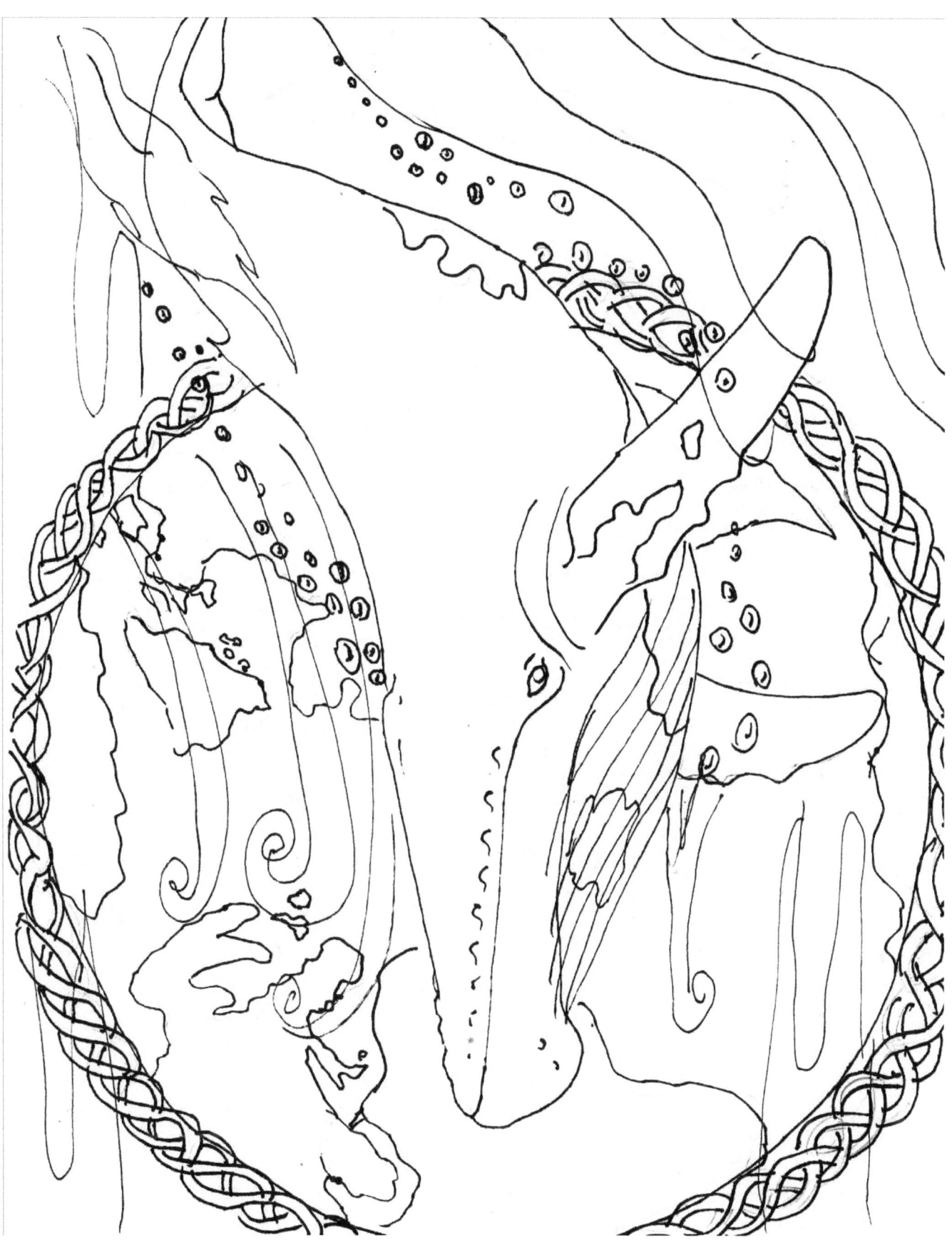

Figure 14 Humpback Whale

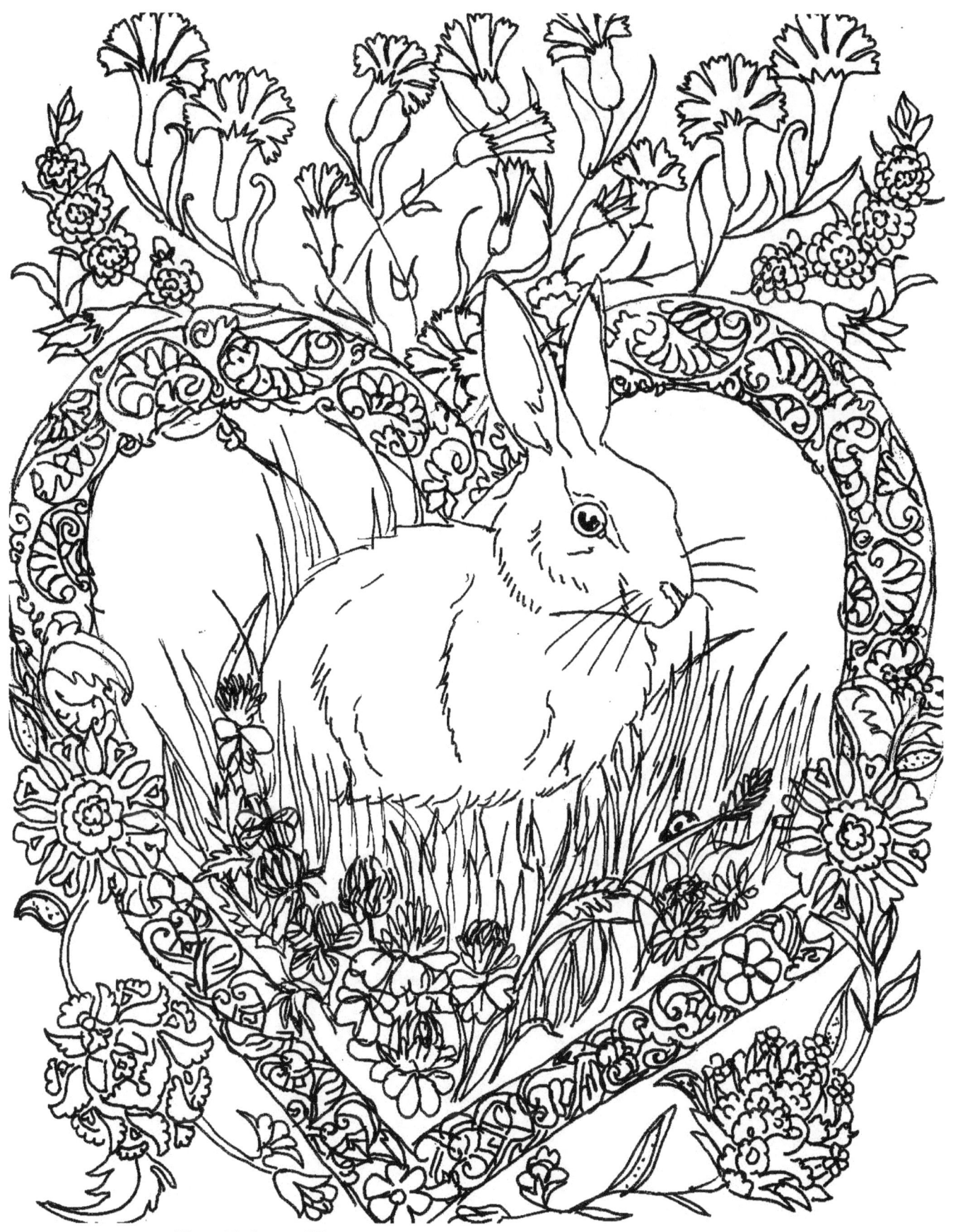

Figure 15 Cottontail Bunny

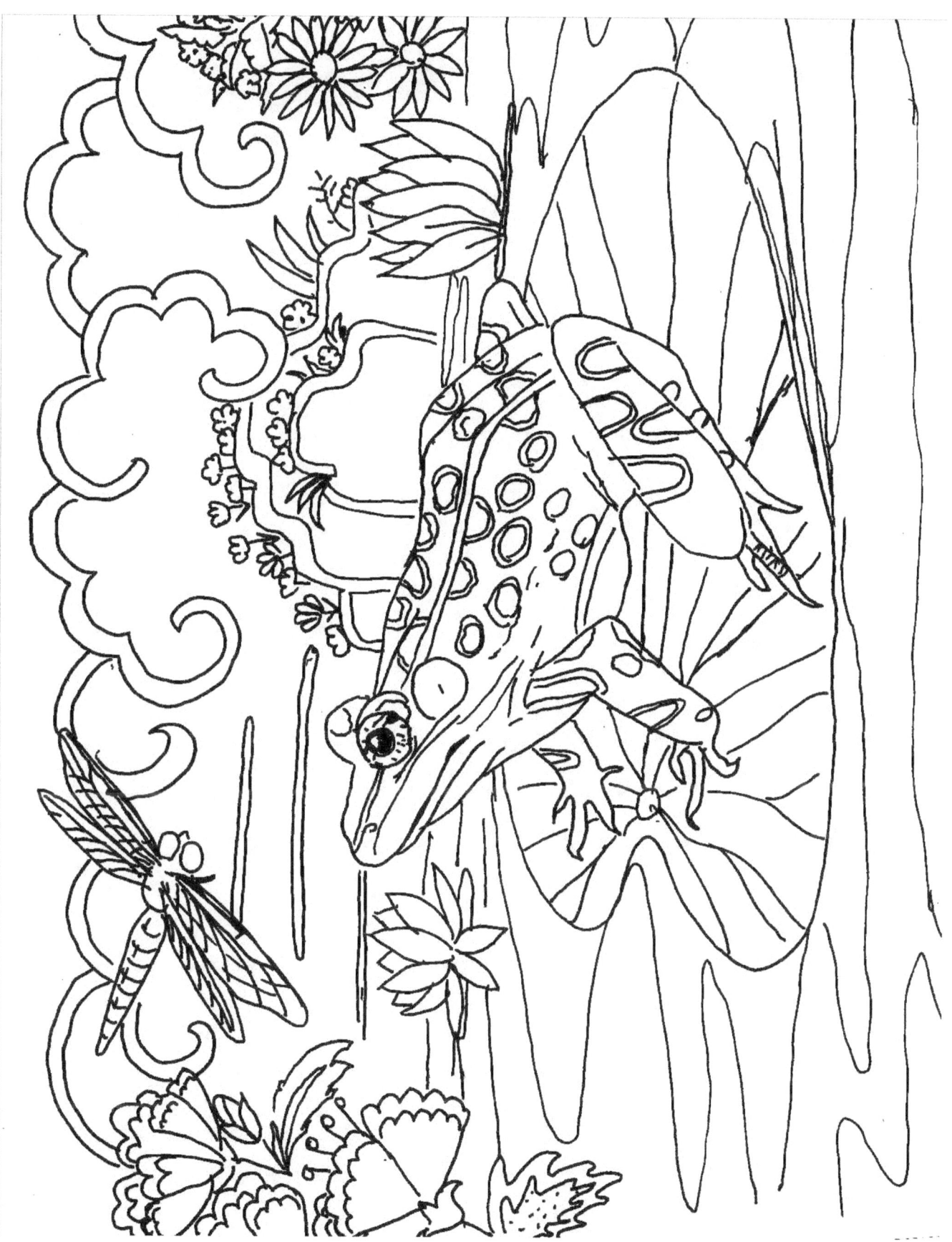

Figure 16 Leopard Frog

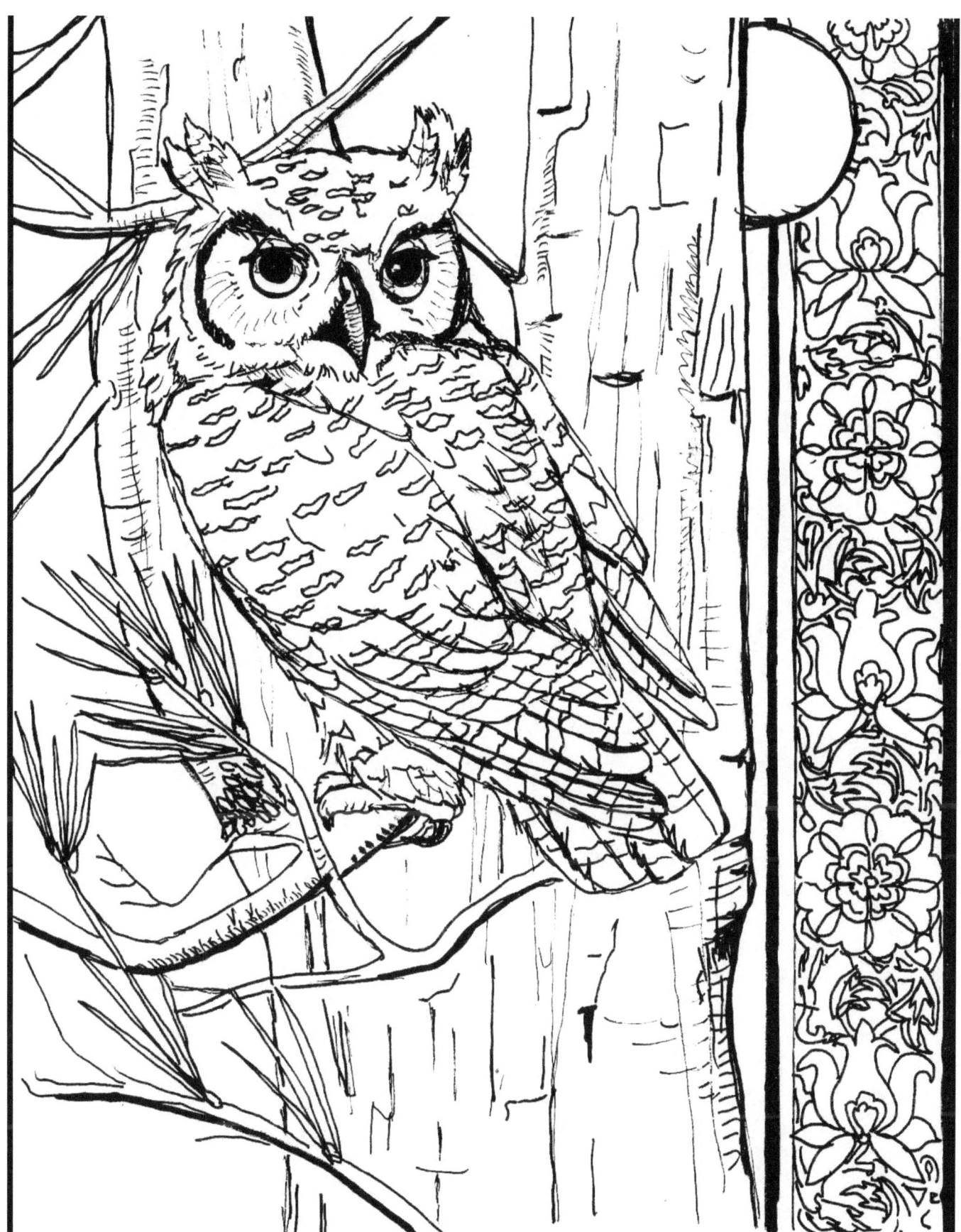

Figure 17 Great Horned Owl

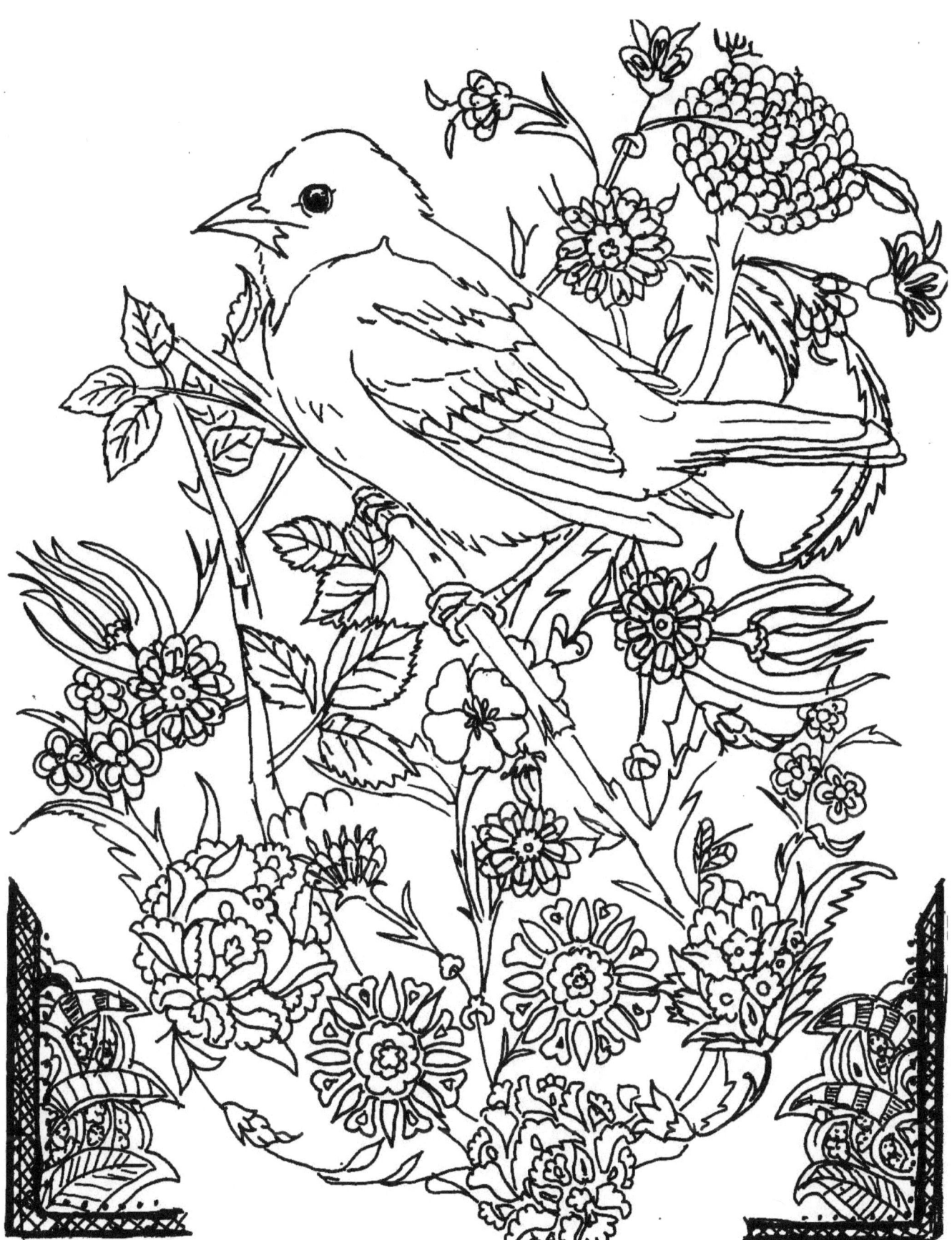

Figure 18 Song Bird

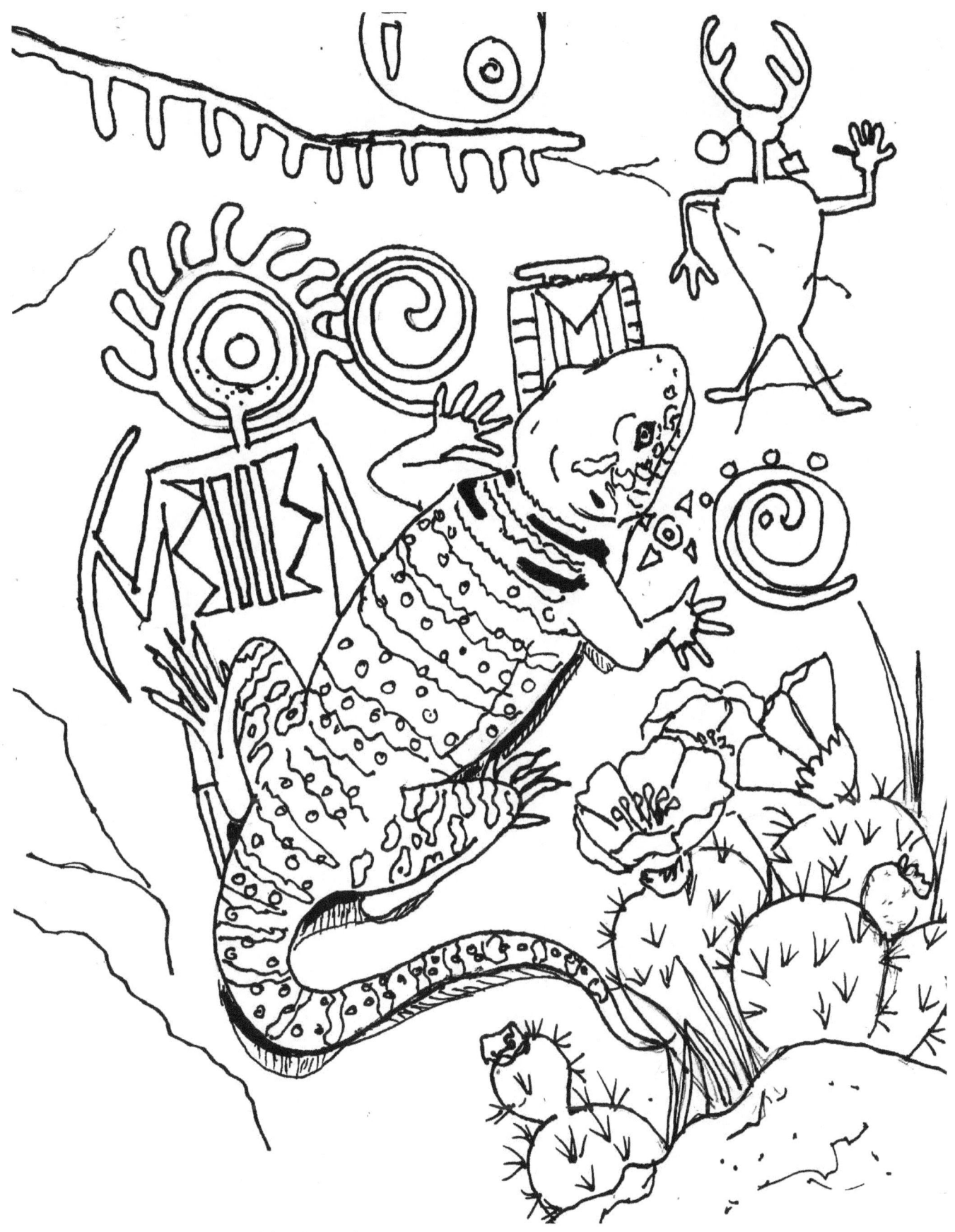

Figure 19 Collared Lizard

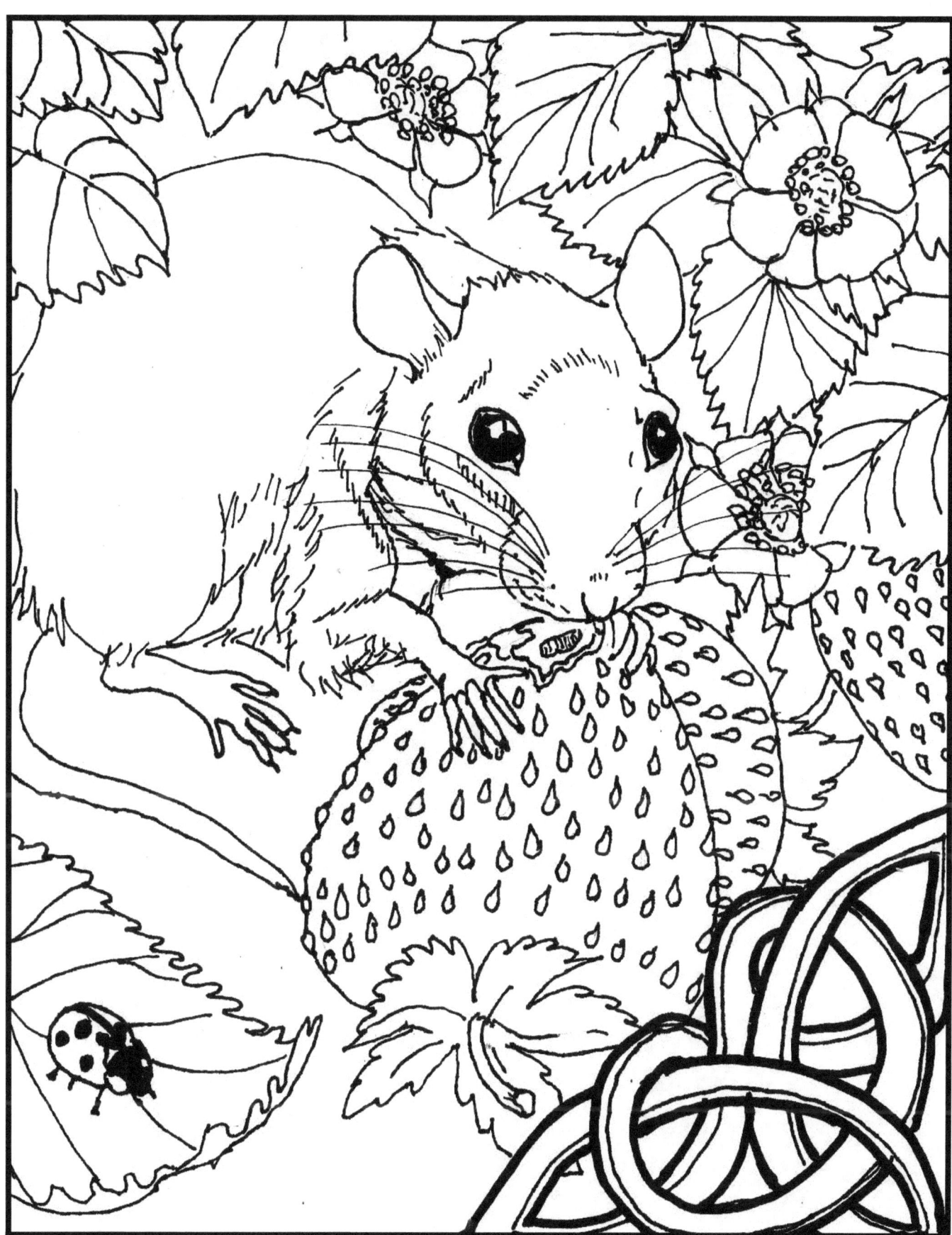

Figure 20 Field Mouse

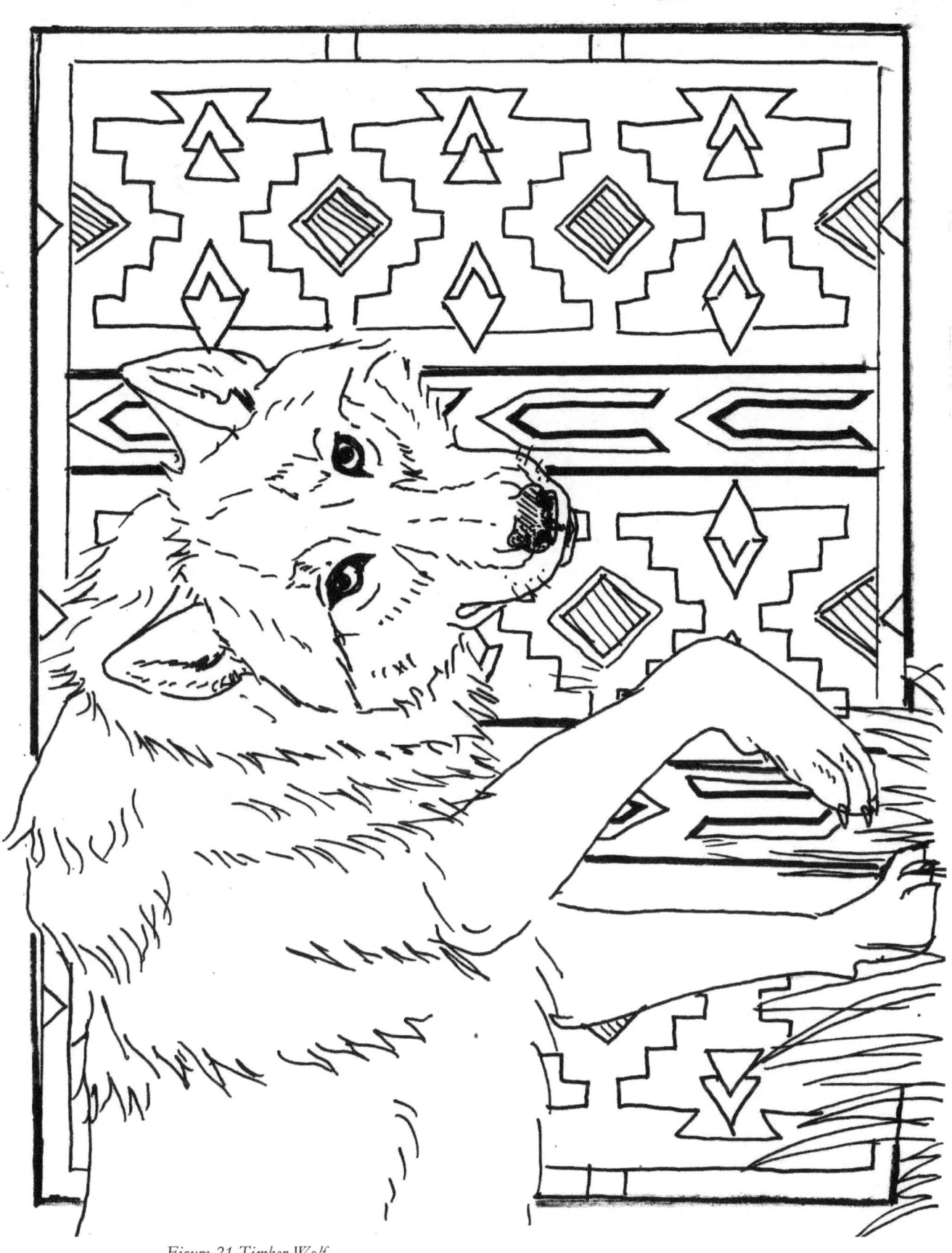

Figure 21 Timber Wolf

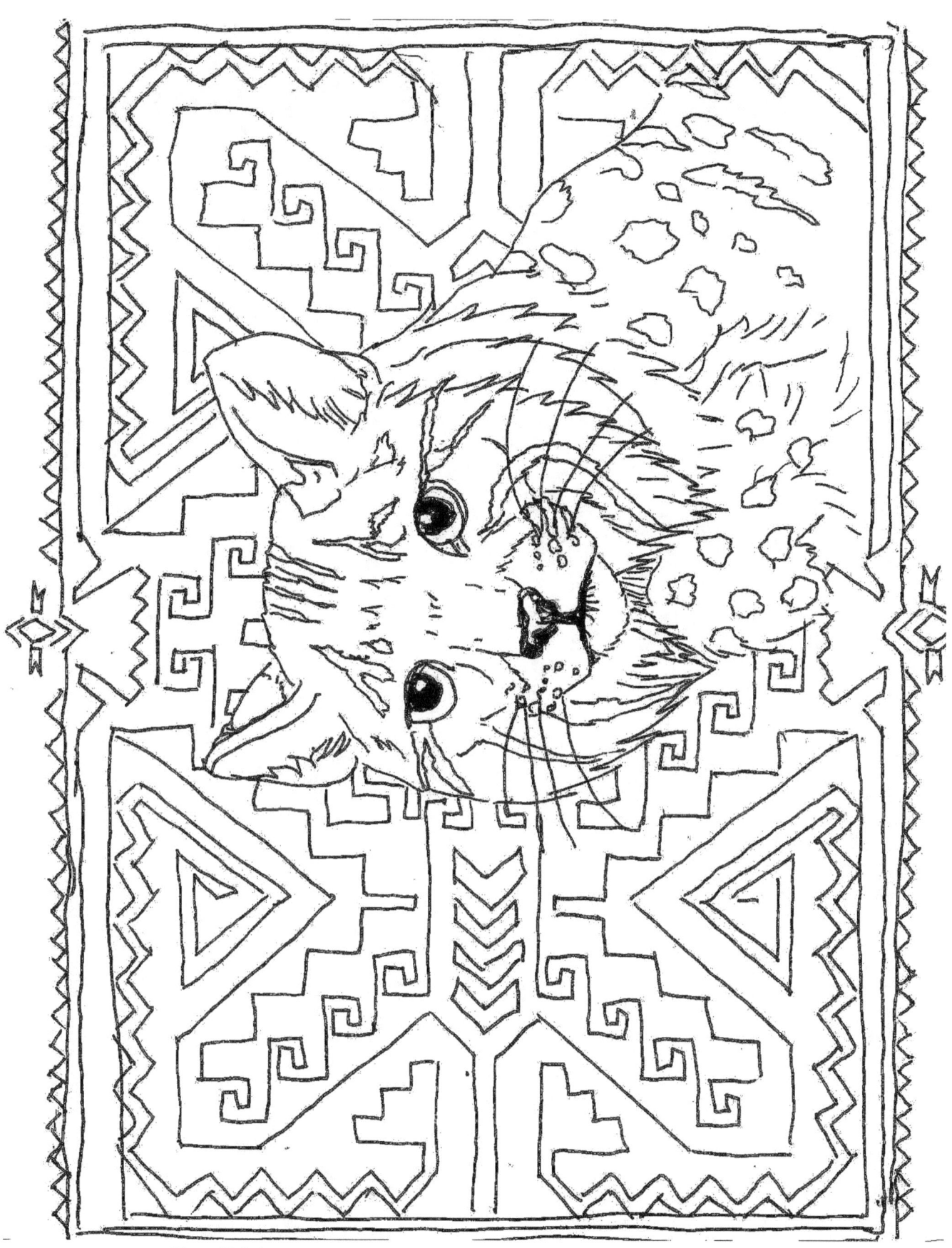

Figure 22 Bobcat

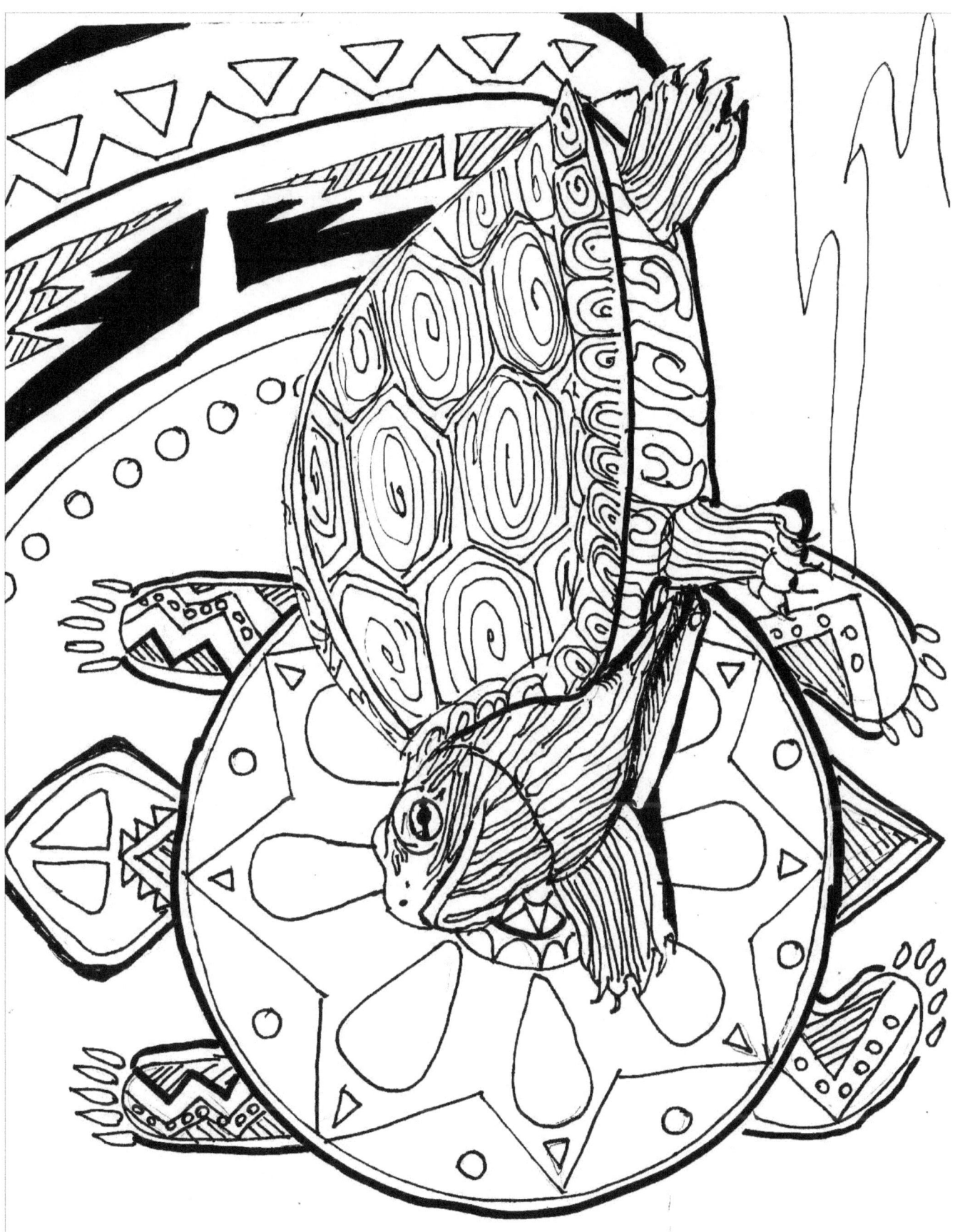

Figure 23 Painted Turtle

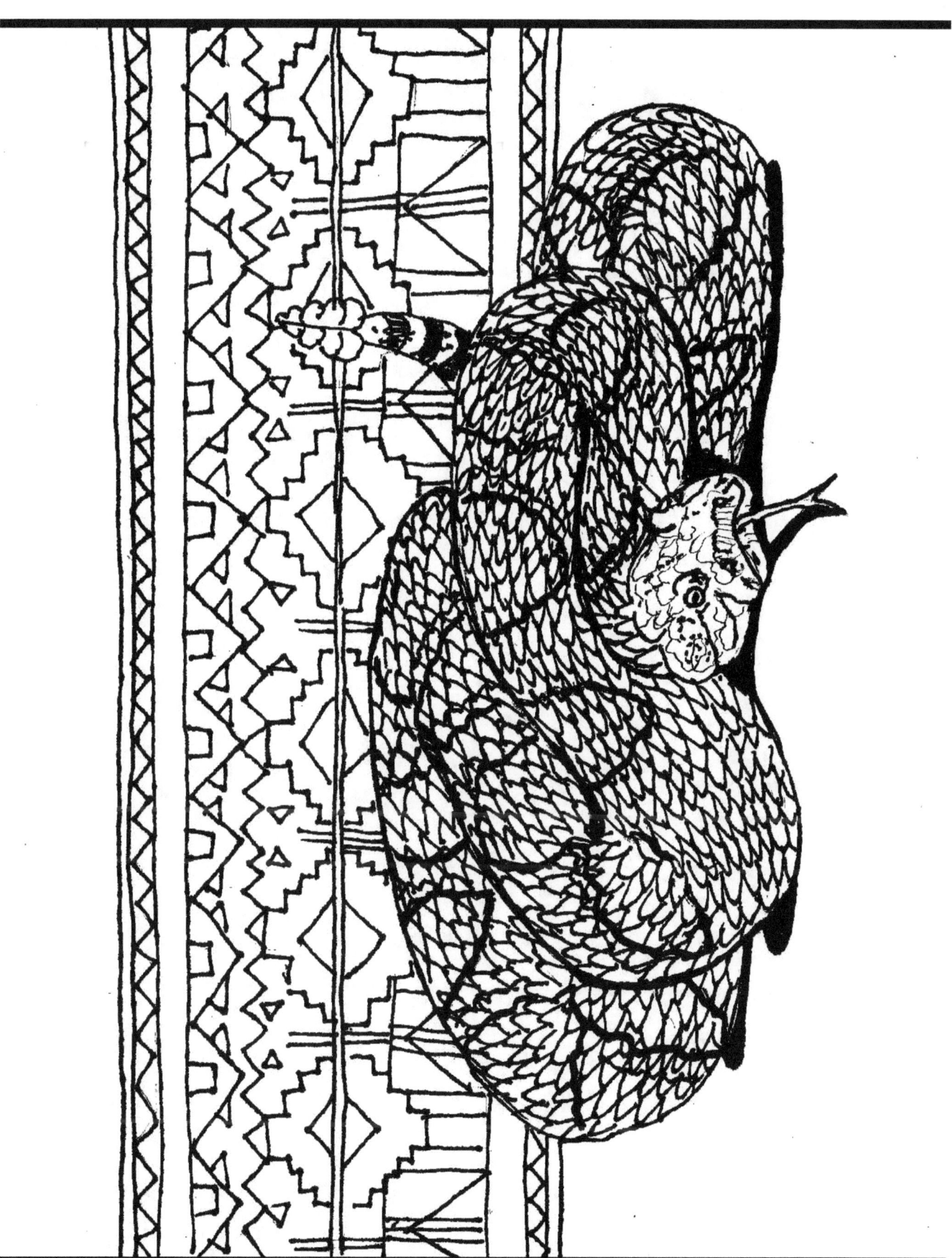

Figure 24 Mojave Green Rattlesnake

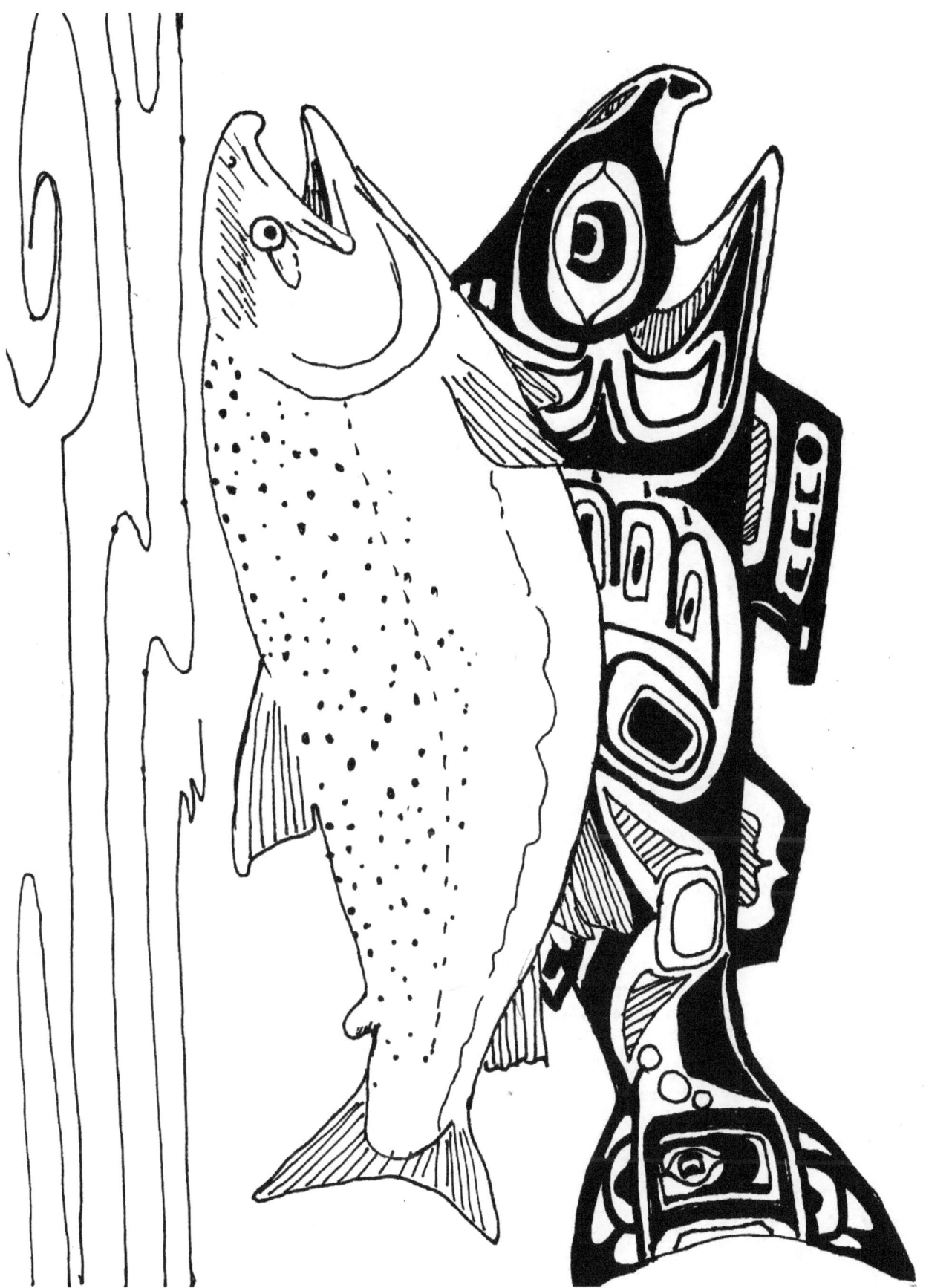

Figure 25 Salmon

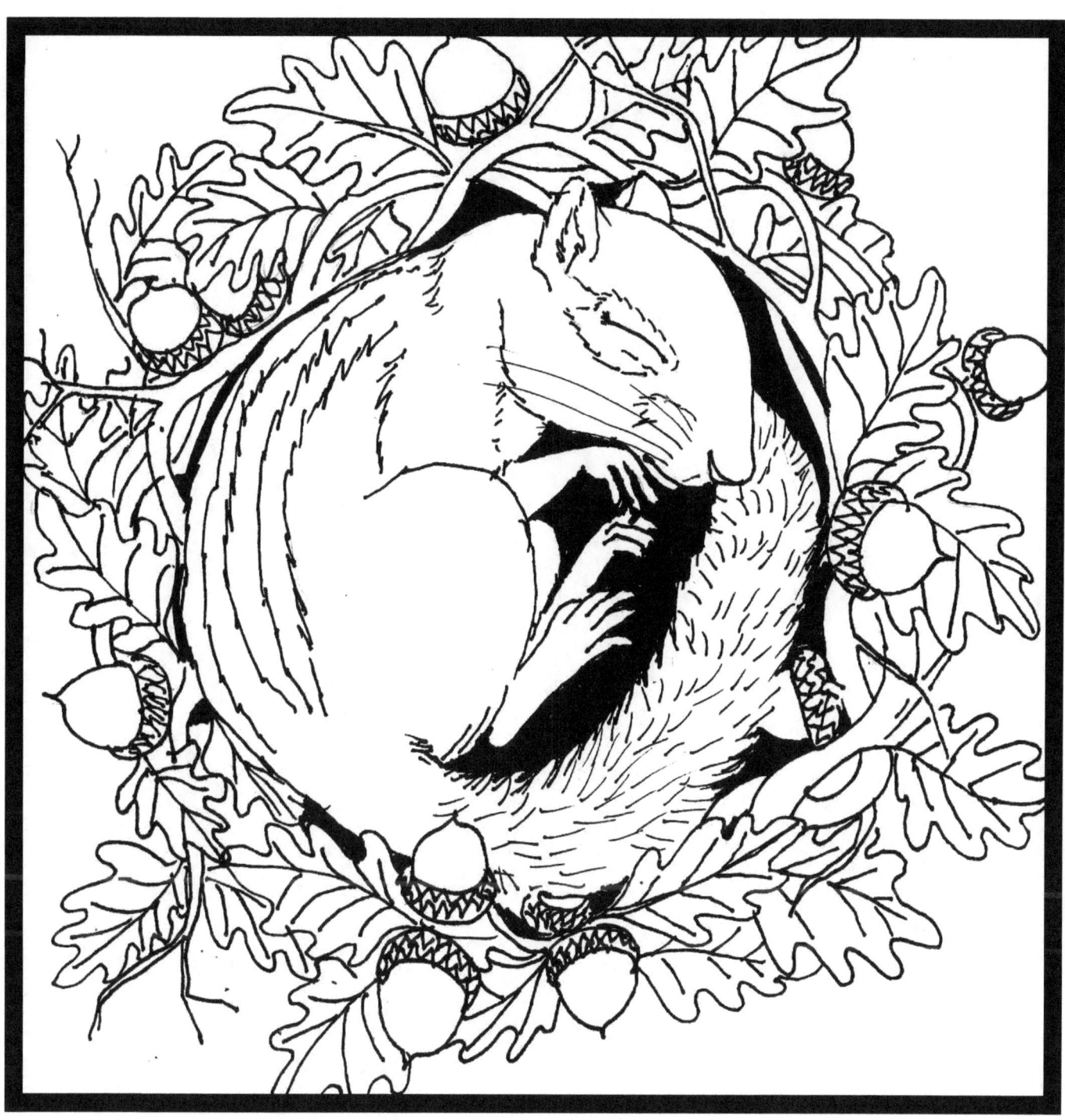

Figure 26 Hibernating Chipmunk

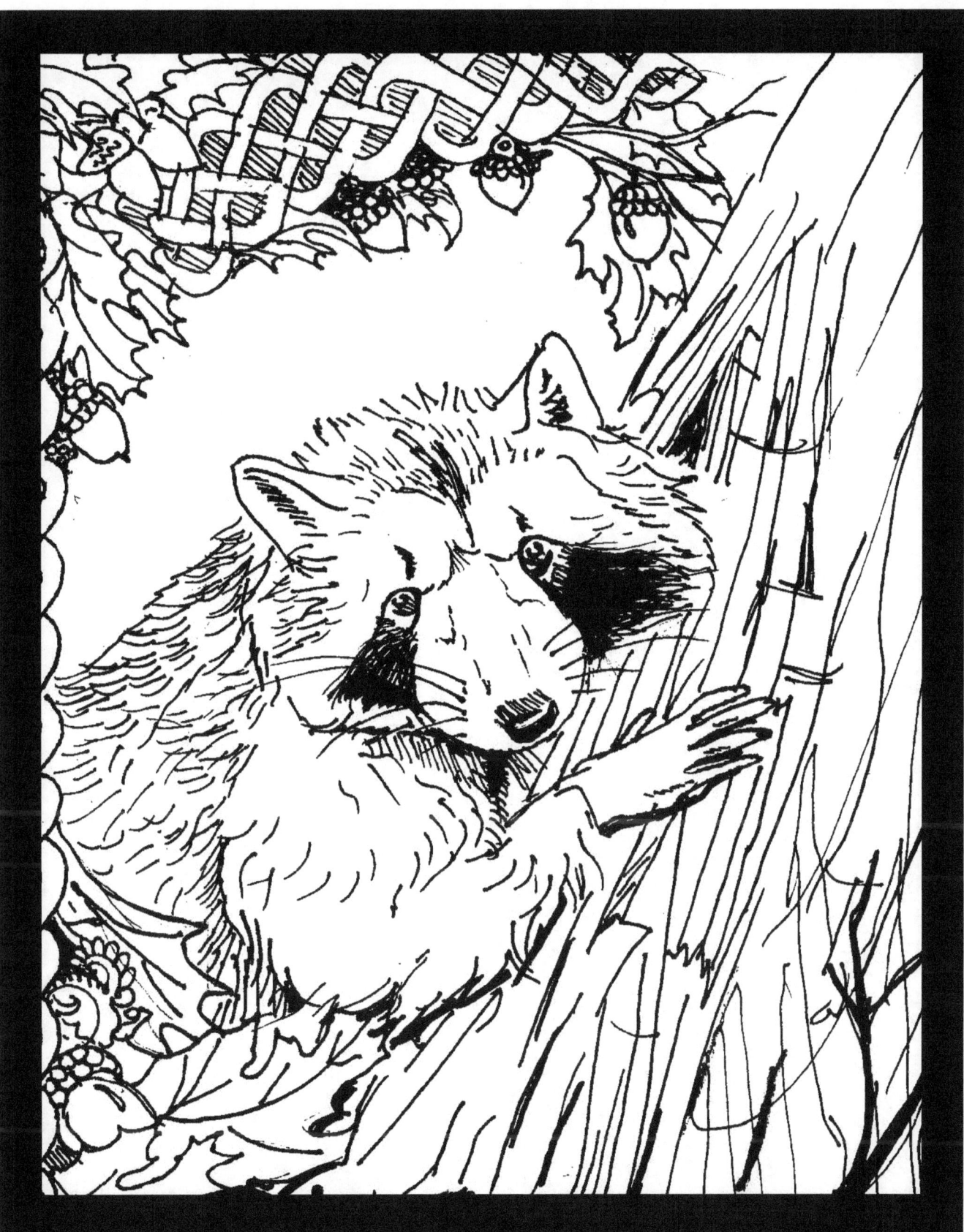

Figure 27 Raccoon

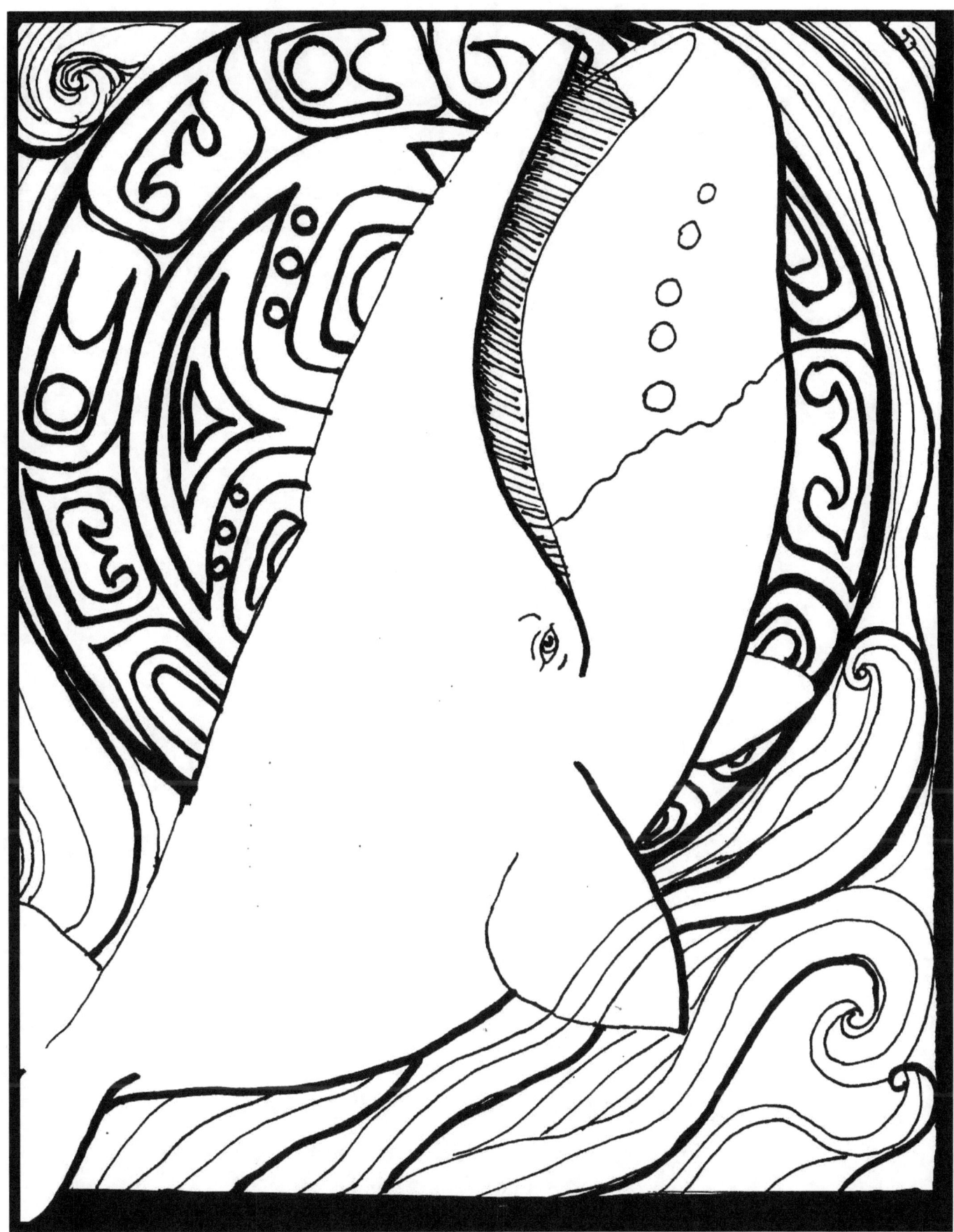

Figure 28 Bowhead Whale

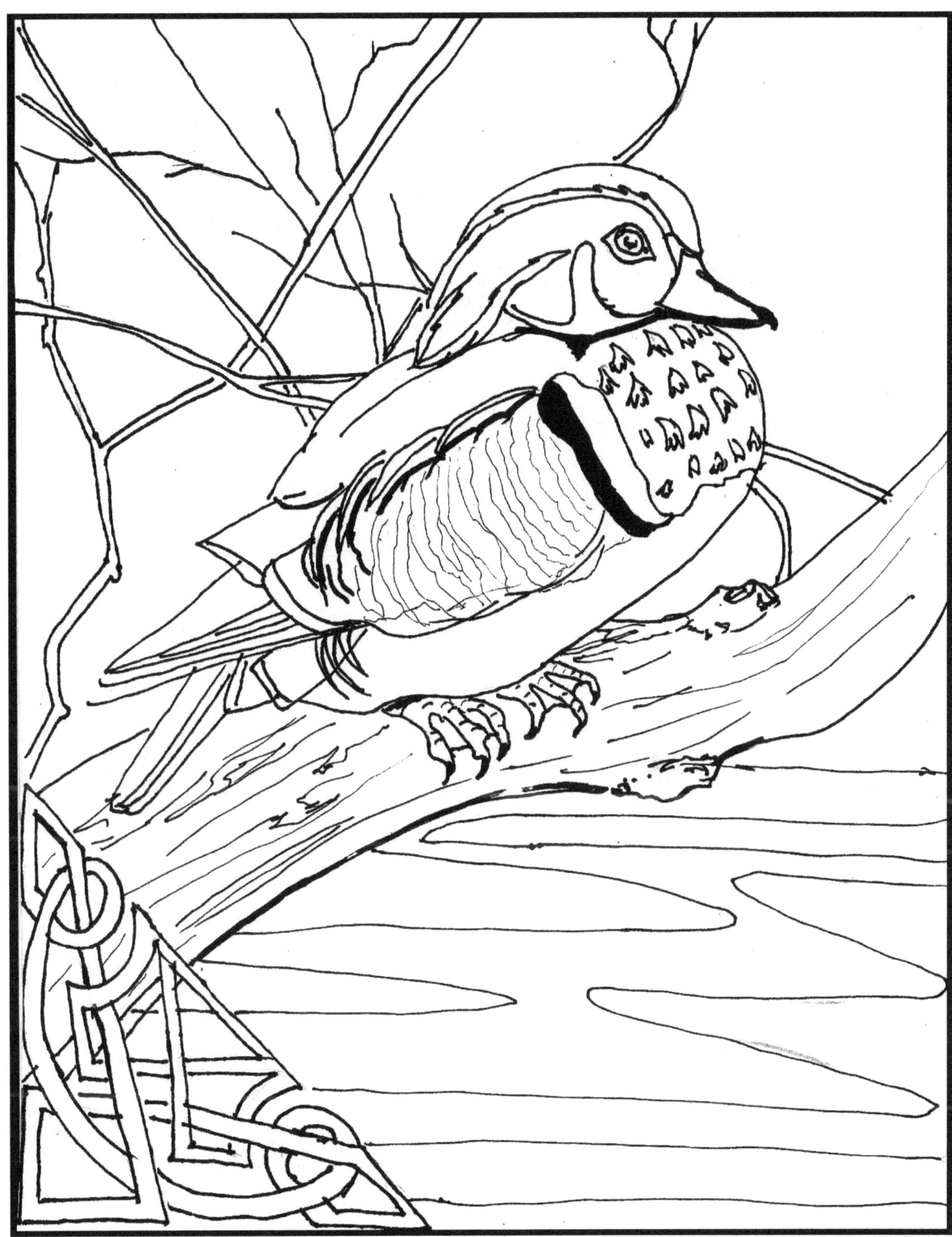

Figure 29 Wood Duck

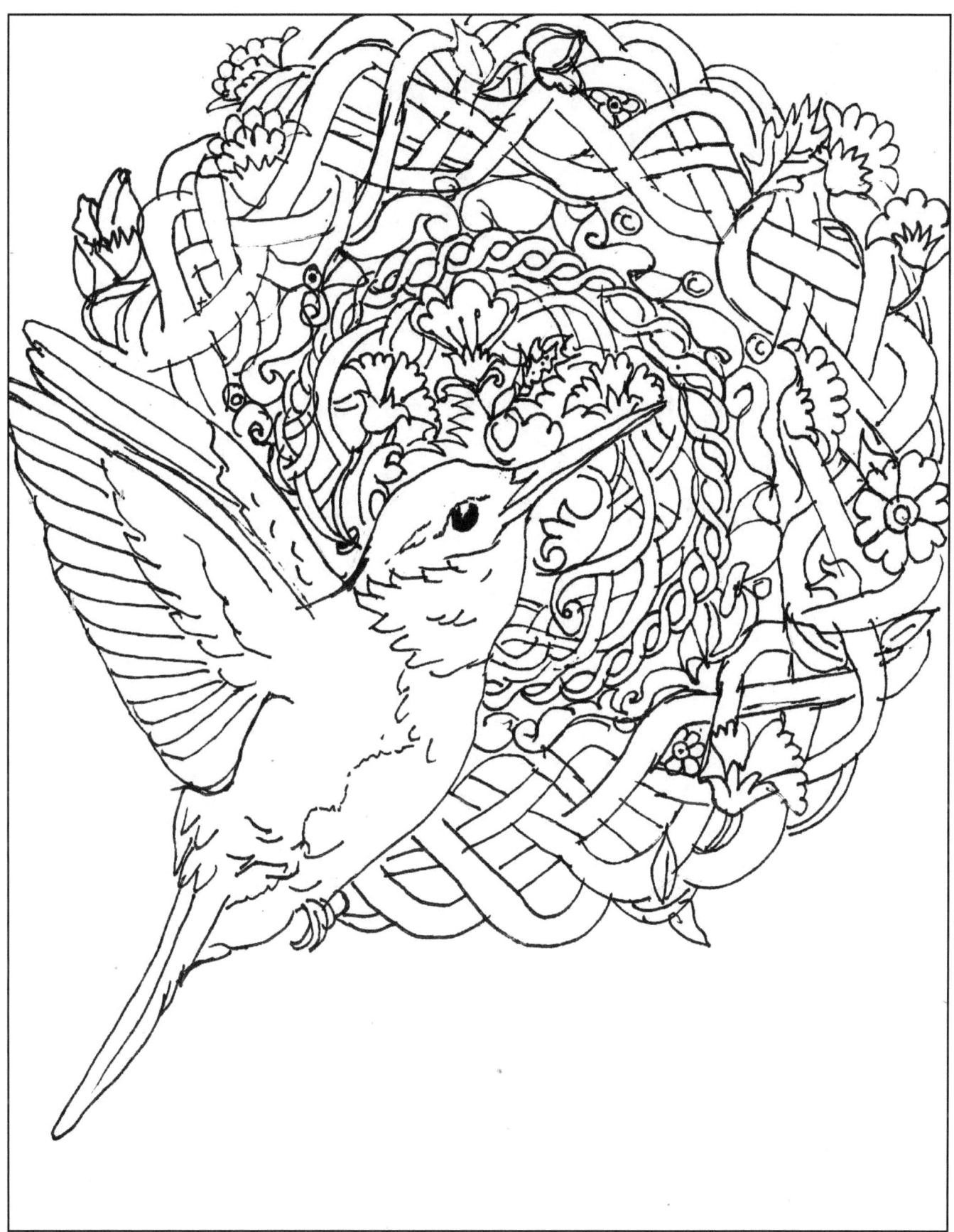

Figure 30 Ruby Throated Hummingbird

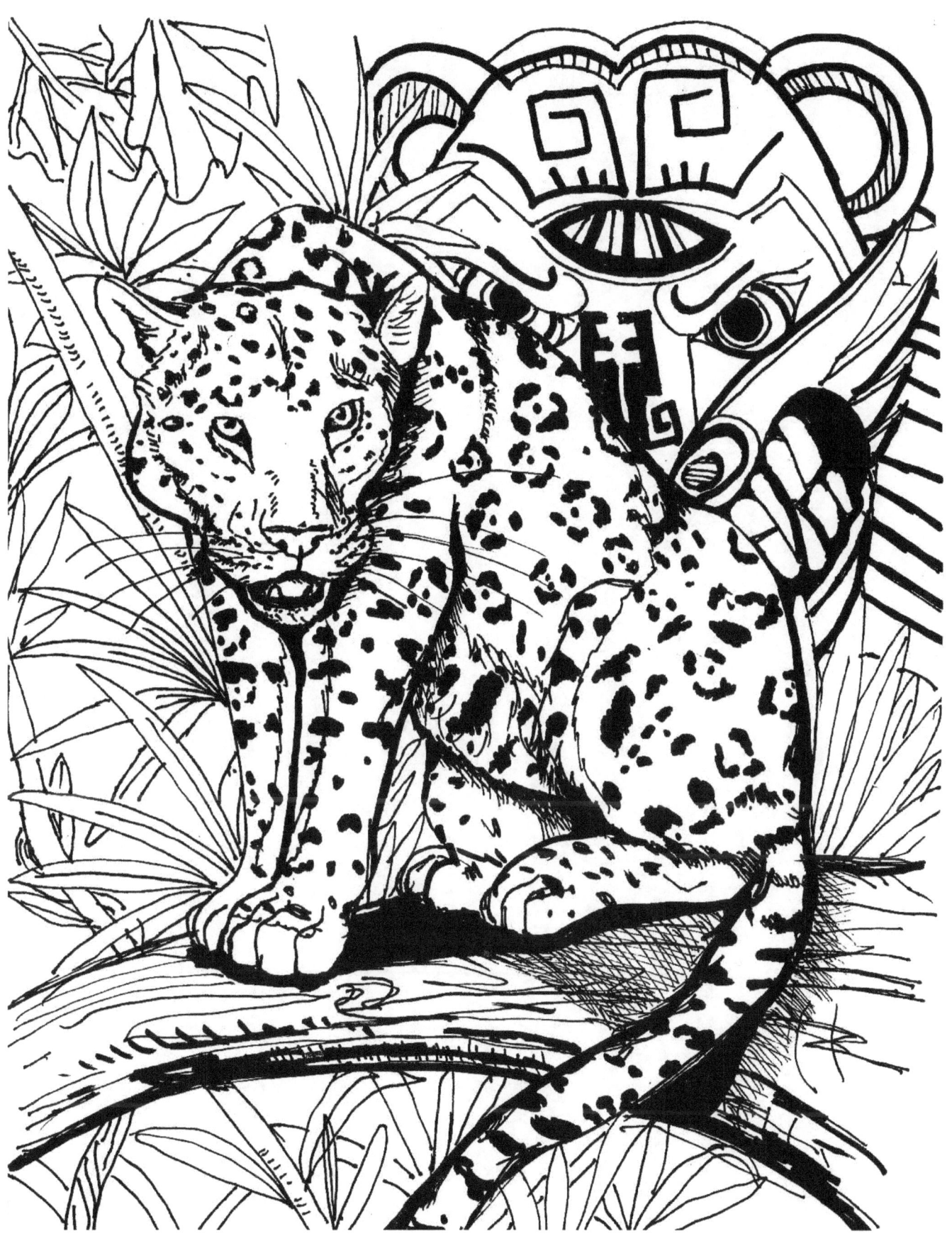

Figure 31 Jaguar

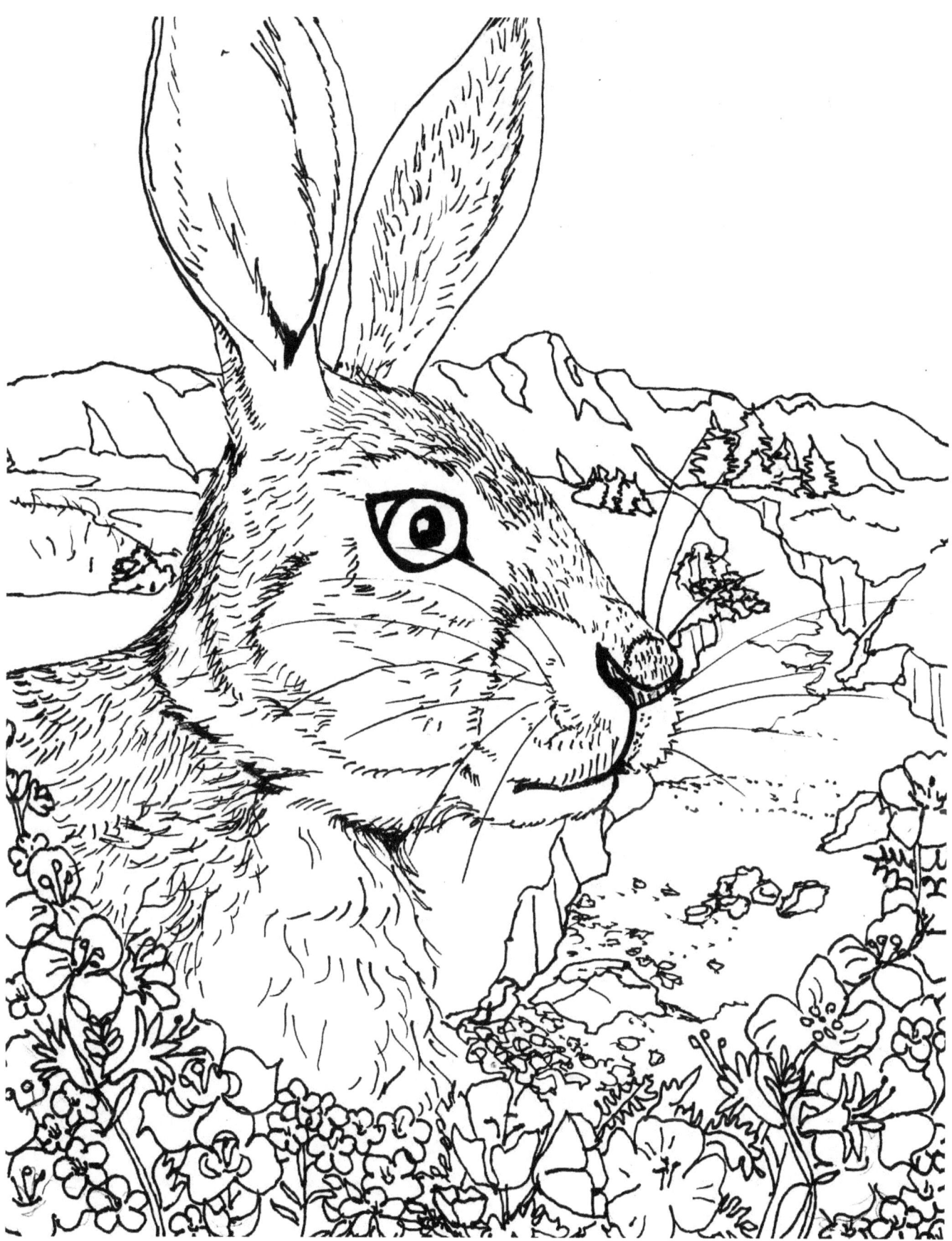

Figure 32 Desert Jack Rabbit

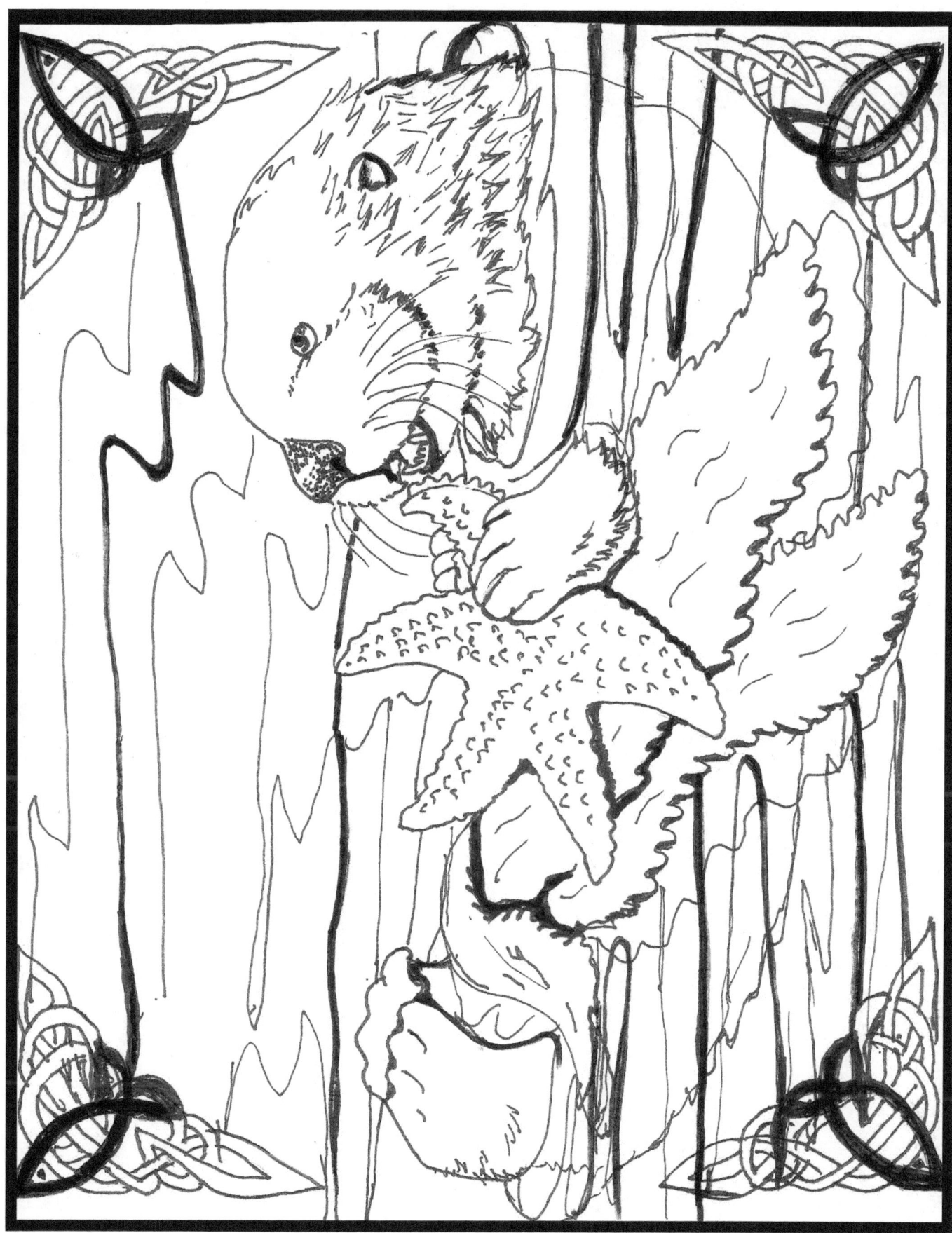

Figure 33 Sea Otter

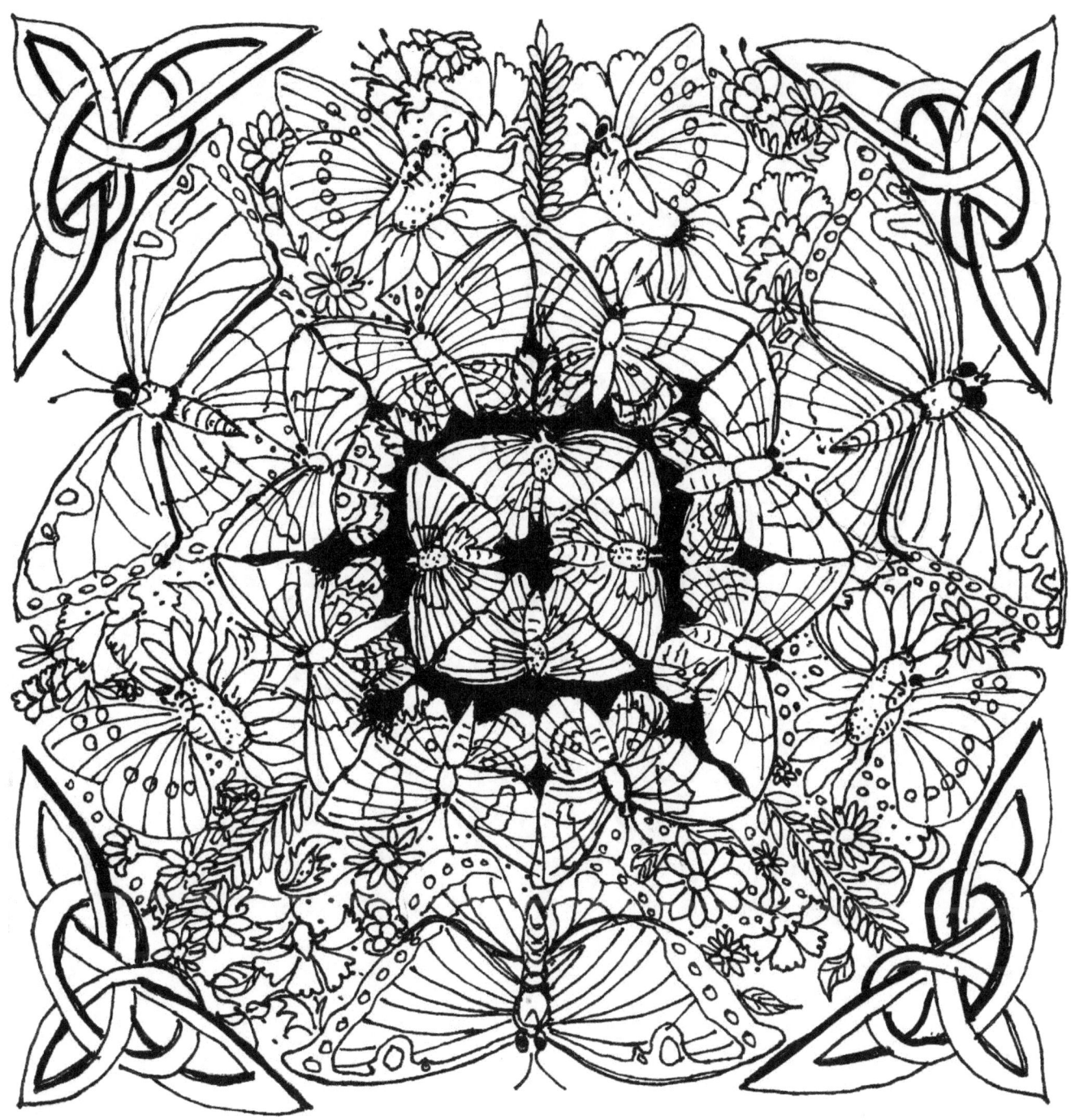

Figure 34 Butterfly Kaleidoscope

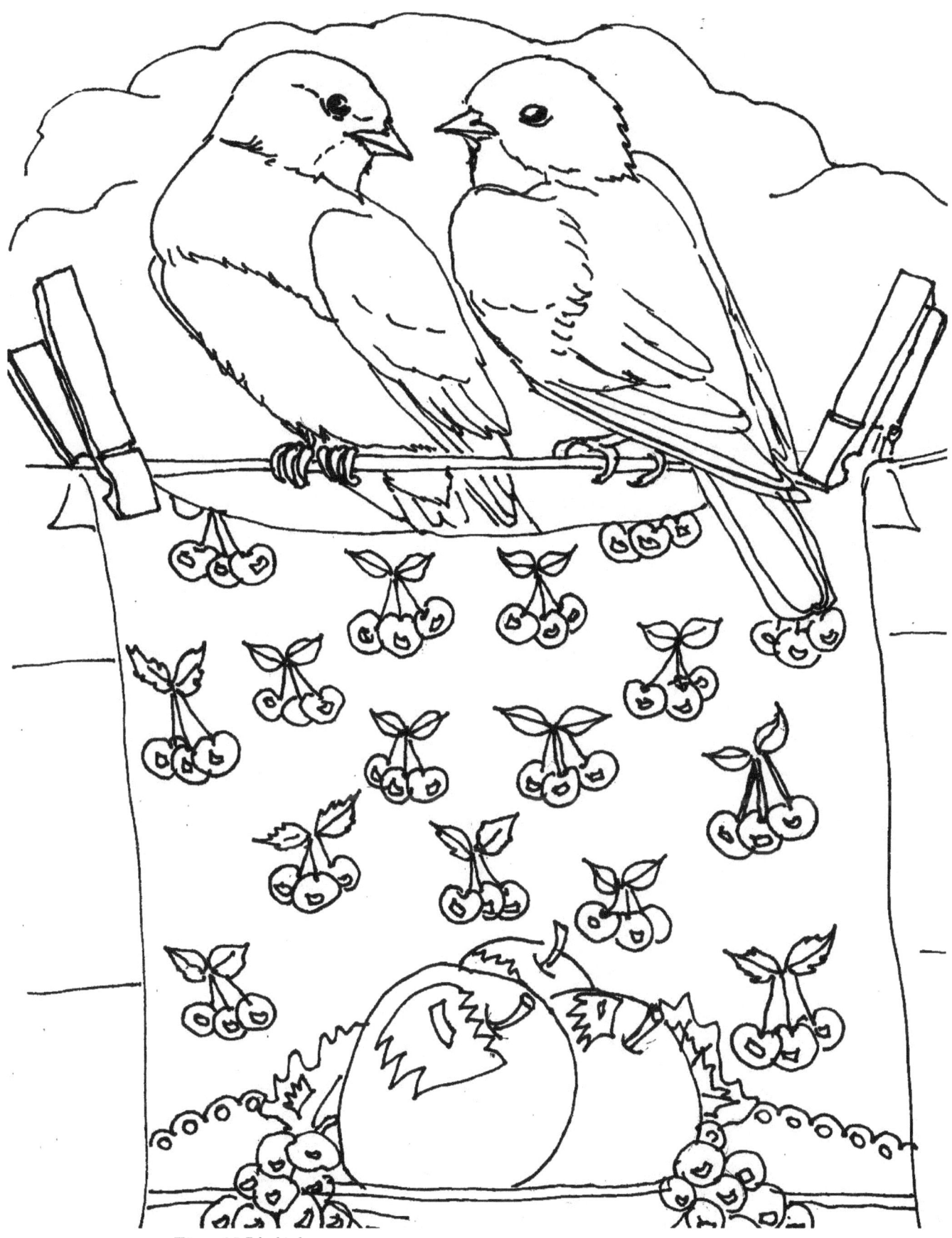

Figure 35 Bluebirds

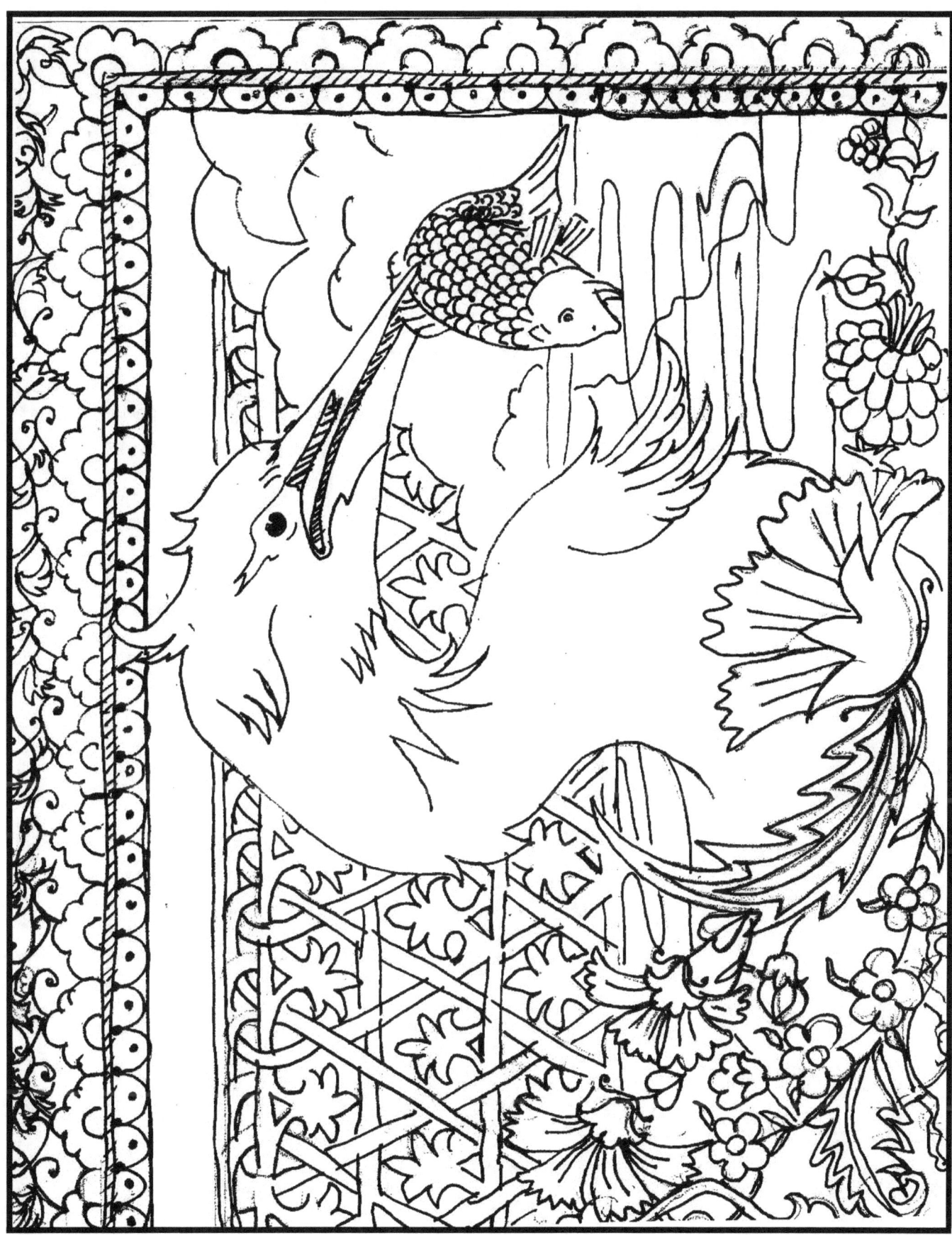

Figure 36 Egret

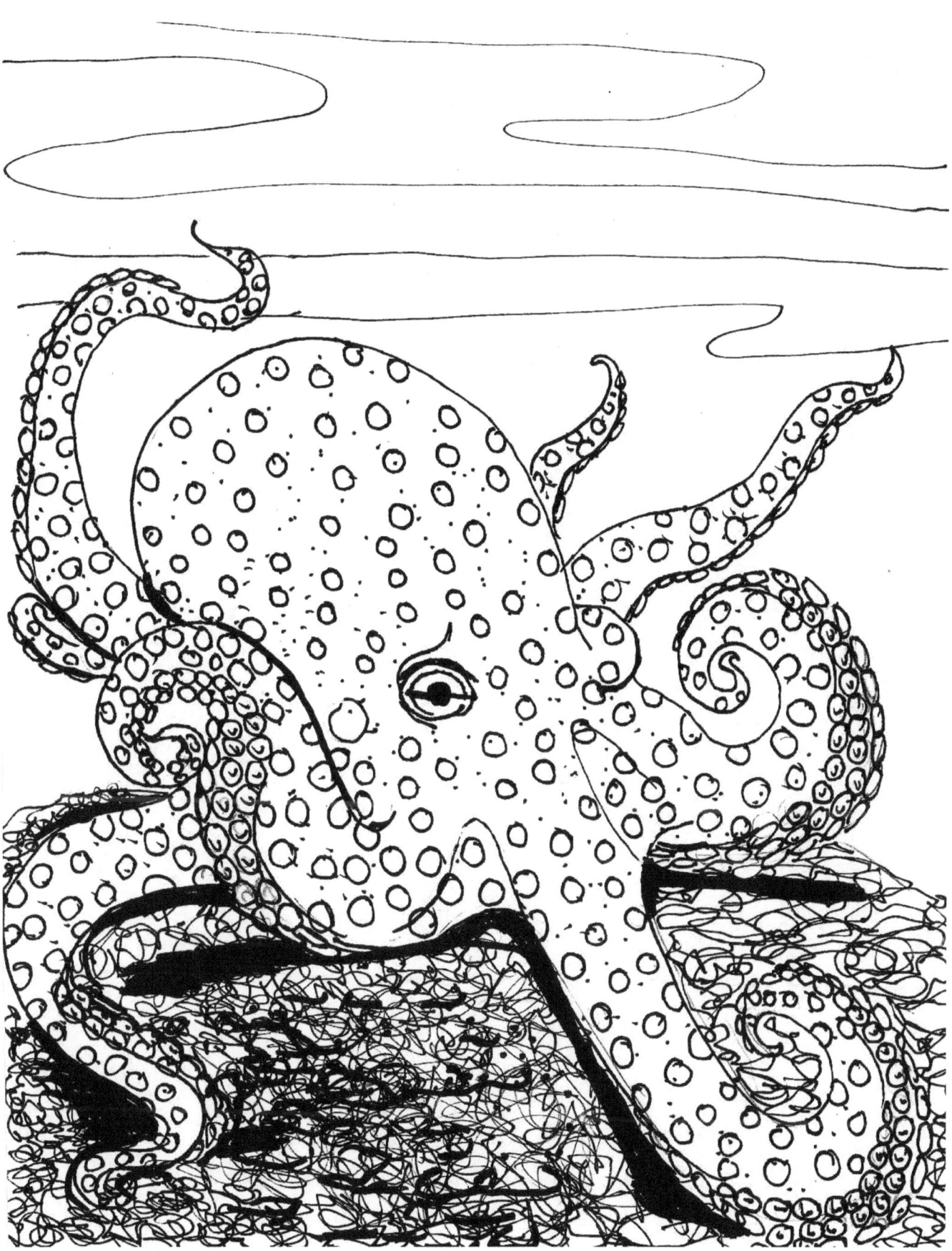

Figure 37 Octopus

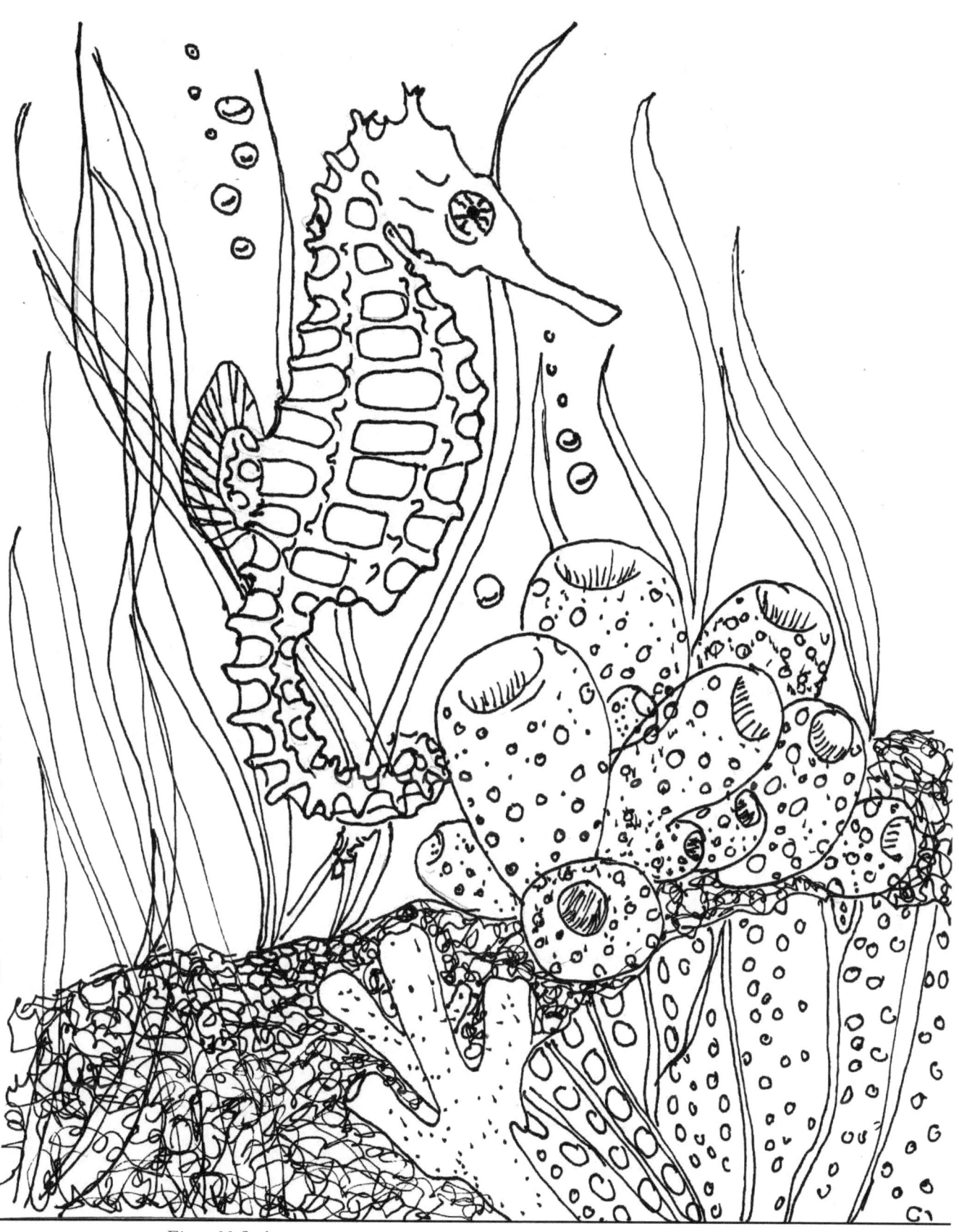

Figure 38 Seahorse

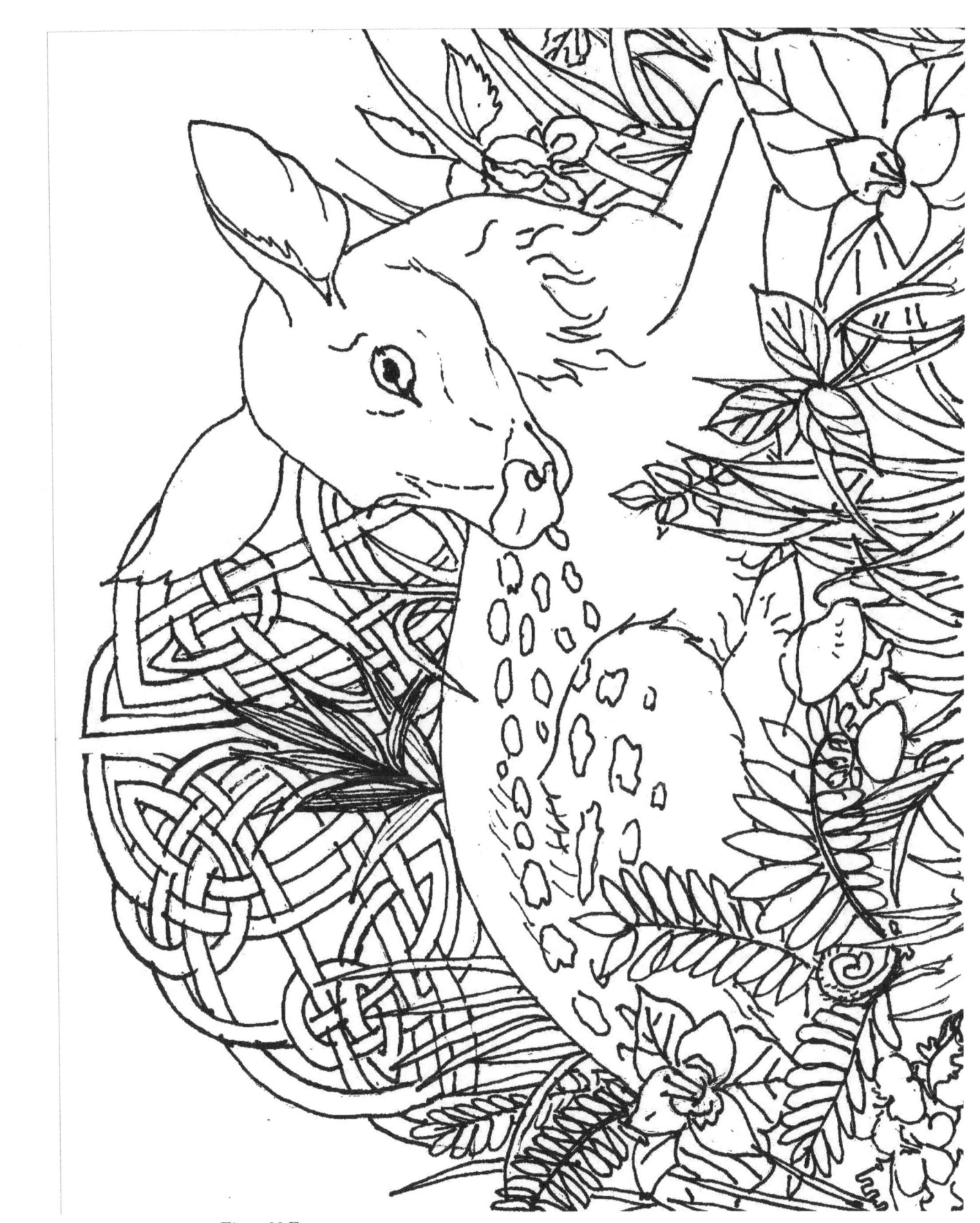

Figure 39 Fawn

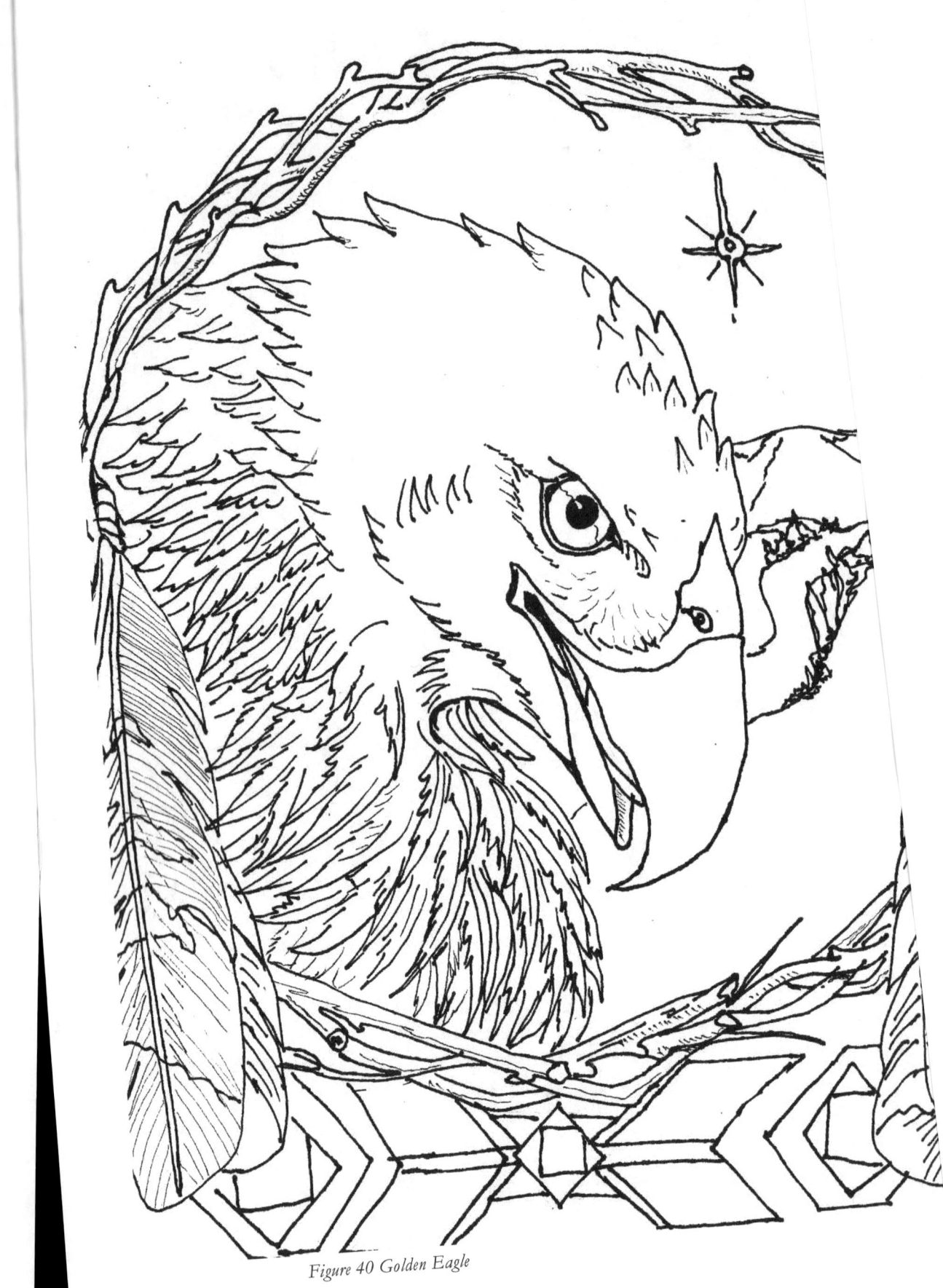

Figure 40 Golden Eagle

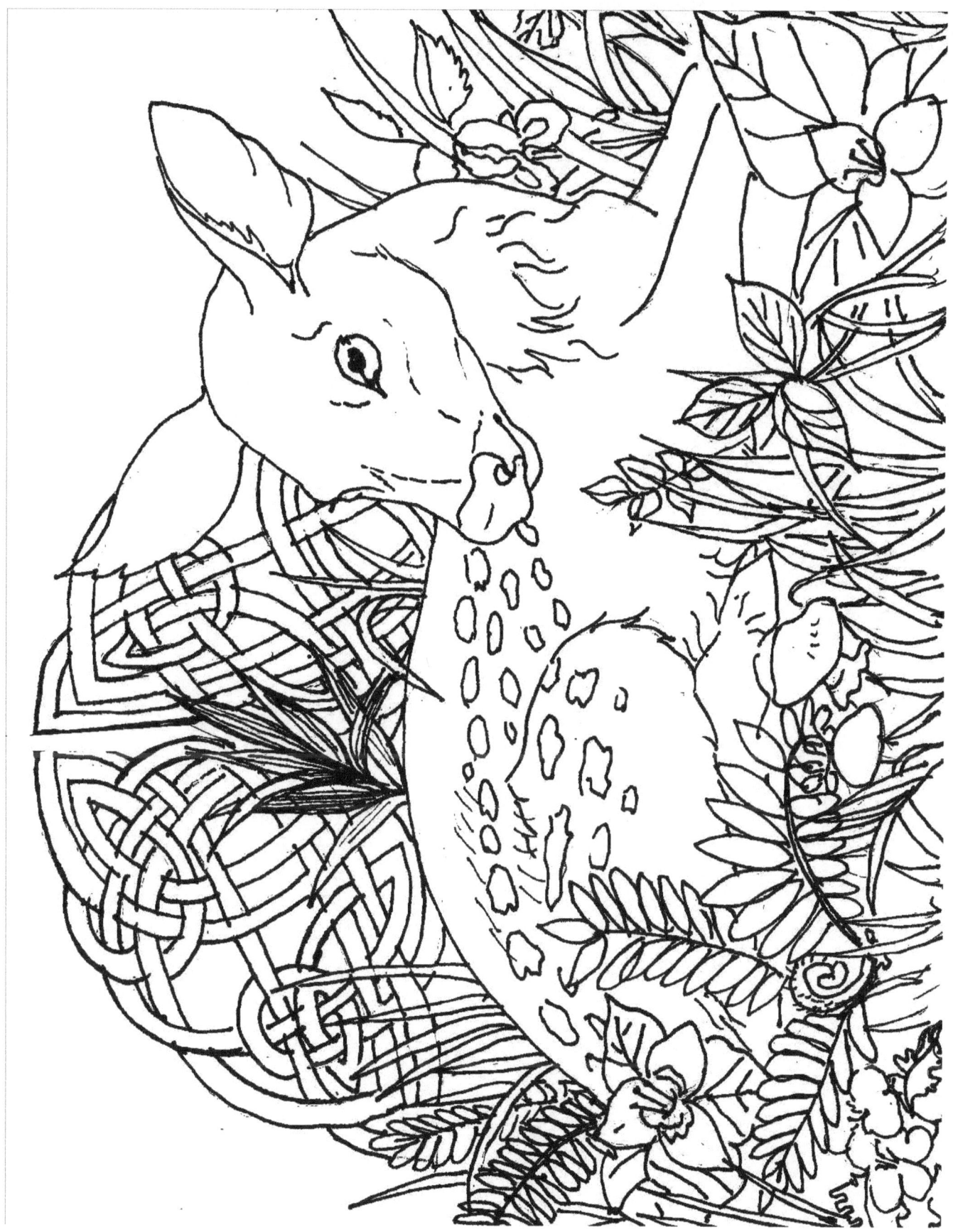

Figure 39 Fawn

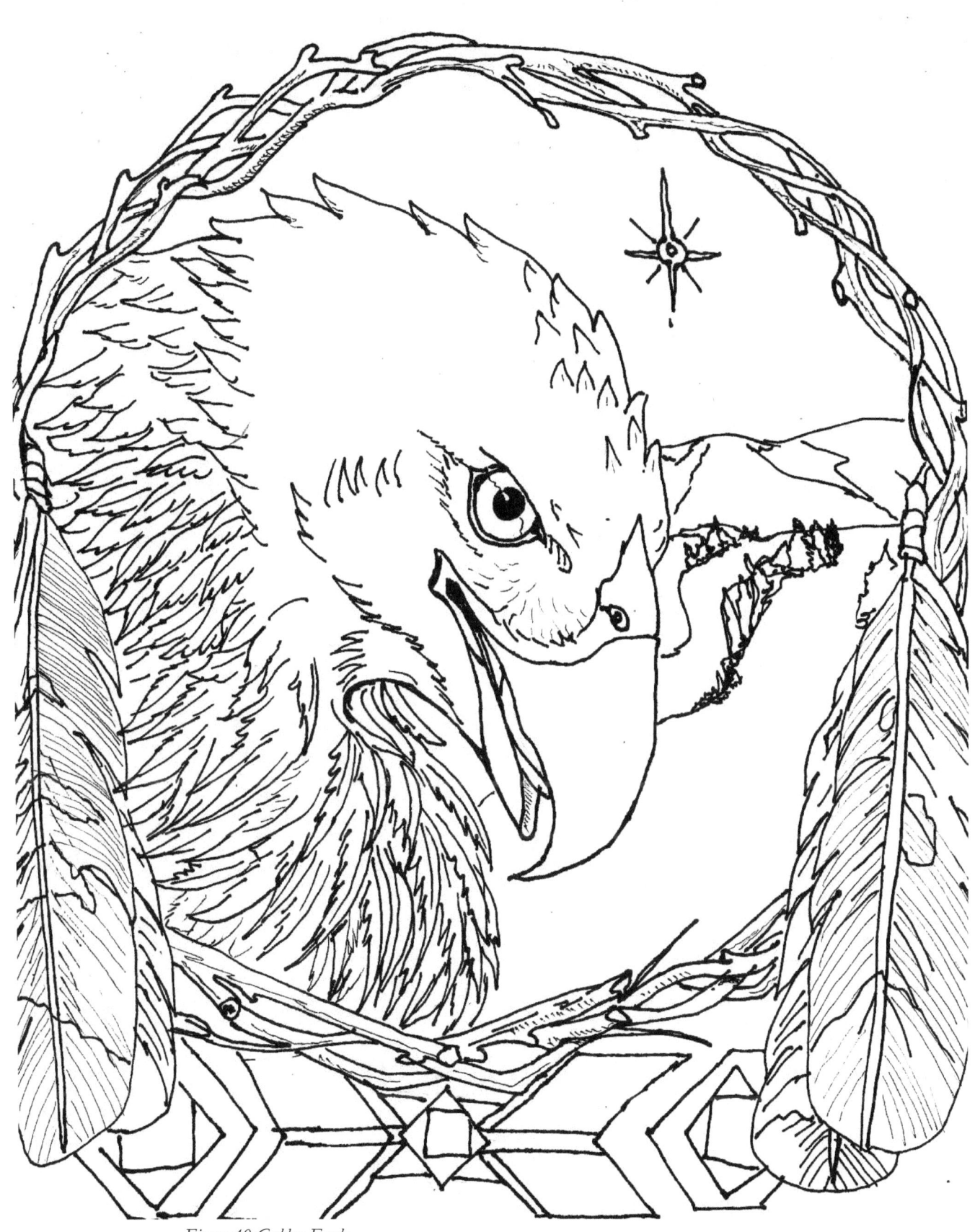

Figure 40 Golden Eagle